Reprints of Economic Classics

A NEGLECTED POINT

IN CONNECTION WITH CRISES

A NEGLECTED POINT IN CONNECTION WITH CRISES

BY

N. JOHANNSEN

[1908]

WITH AN INTRODUCTORY NOTE

N. A. L. J. JOHANNSEN: AMATEUR ECONOMIST

BY JOSEPH DORFMAN

REPRINTS OF ECONOMIC CLASSICS

AUGUSTUS M. KELLEY · PUBLISHERS

NEW YORK 1971

First Edition 1908

(New York: The Bankers Publishing Company, 1908)

REPRINTED 1971 BY

AUGUSTUS M. KELLEY • PUBLISHERS

REPRINTS OF ECONOMIC CLASSICS

New York New York 10001

I S B N 0-678-00759-4

L C N 78-129861

PRINTED IN THE UNITED STATES OF AMERICA

by SENTRY PRESS, NEW YORK, N. Y. 10019

NICHOLAS AUGUST LUDWIG JACOB JOHANNSEN: THE "AMATEUR ECONOMIST"[1]

N. Johannsen (1844-1928) of New York presented one of the sharpest critiques of the doctrine of savings in its relation to depressions. Heretofore little has been known of him, yet some of the ideas he expounded contained the germs of modern developments.[2] Perhaps this can be accounted for by the fact that Johannsen was one of the strangest characters in American economics. He was of German birth and retained a keen interest in German matters, publishing in German as well as in English. He had little formal education. For many years he was an executive with a New York export and import firm, and his letter books indicate that he engaged extensively, and rather successfully, in stock-market operations. Johannsen's first writings appear under pseudonyms, a fact which he explained on the ground that his employer might think that he could not pay full attention to business and write on financial topics at one and the same time.

Johannsen began writing as early as 1878, publishing a pamphlet, *Cheap Capital,* under the pseudonym "A. Merwin." In this he stated that depression hung on because business could not obtain "cash capital" or "cash funds" at low interest rates. The depression, therefore,

---

[1] Reprinted with minor changes from Joseph Dorfman, *The Economic Mind in American Civilization,* 5 volumes (1946-1959; New York: Augustus M. Kelley Publishers, 1966-1969) III, pp. 408-413; IV, p. 15.

For additional light on Johannsen, see Joseph Dorfman's introductory essay "Some Documentary Notes on the Relations Among J. M. Clark, N. A. L. J. Johannsen and J. M. Keynes" in reprint, Clark, *The Costs of the World War [I] to the American People* (1931; New York: Augustus M. Kelley Publishers, 1970).

[2] The author obtained personal items and letters from Johannsen's stepson, W. H. Seiler.

could be alleviated if the withdrawal of greenbacks were stopped, but in the end the increase in amount of greenbacks could not achieve prosperity, for greenbacks had no adequate security behind them. Rather, cash capital should be expanded through the increase of national bank notes backed by government bonds, these notes to be redeemable in greenbacks. While such expansion was inflationary, he contended that it would be safe if it were continued until the long-term rate of interest fell to approximately 2½ or 3 per cent.

A rather interesting point was Johannsen's presentation of the *modus operandi* of panics. If all property were owned free of debt, he said, the pressure to sell, characteristic of panics, would not occur. However, since most property was encumbered with debt, in many cases nearly to its full value, any decline in price, started by the most casual occurrence or some important event, would eliminate the margin owned by the nominal owner of the property, thus forcing its sale. This process originated in the stock exchange and spread to all other property.

Around the turn of the century Johannsen began working on a theory of depression that constituted a significant contribution to the literature. In 1908, at the age of sixty-four, he published his basic theory, *A Neglected Point in Connection with Crises.* In this work, and later in the condensed pamphlet *Business Depressions* (1925), he argued that the true cause of depressions was in an "'impaired' form of savings." Primarily and immediately, by reducing demand, the act of saving tended to create unemployment. When, however, savings were invested in productive equipment or other durable wealth, full employment resulted, and such use of savings constituted "normal" savings. He used as an example a community with an income of $100,000,000, of which he assumed that 85 per cent was expended for consumables and 15 per cent for investment in the construction of new productive equipment. About 85 per cent of the population, then, were engaged in producing consumables for all, while the 15 per cent saved went to "the constructive workers" as income for their services and for the production of the raw materials. Thus all workers were fully employed.

"Impair savings" differed from "normal" savings, he wrote, in that while the latter when disbursed came to the receivers in the form of earnings, the impair savings came to them "over the bridge of their own impoverishment." Suppose of the $100,000,000 of the community's total annual earnings, 15 per cent had no opportunity for useful investment, there being already "productive capital in the community up to the satiation point, sufficient to produce all consumptibles" for which there was a sale. Then the constructive workers who ordinarily earned $15,000,000 in the aggregate remained unemployed. These workers would be forced to meet their living expenses by using up their savings accounts, selling their securities, taking mortgages on their homes, or borrowing from friends.

The saver, then, had extracted money from the community as income, but had been unable to return it to the community. His savings thus became "impair" savings. Should he subsequently return the funds either through extending loans or purchasing the properties of needy people, his investments would become "impair investments." These loans and purchases would bring partial relief, but only after his savings had caused unemployment, retrenchment, and destitution. Johannsen's analysis was unique in that it demonstrated a peculiar multiplication of this primary cause, achieved by the reaction of one trade upon another. This principle Johannsen called the "multiplying (or cumulative) principle" and originally presented it in 1903 in his brochure *Depressions-Perioden,* published under the pseudonym J. J. O. Lahne. In *A Neglected Point* Johannsen explained that the baneful effects of impair savings extended beyond those who ordinarily constructed the new capital goods, for unemployment in these lines would reduce the demand for consumable goods, thus creating further unemployment. One group of workers after another would be affected until finally even the incomes of the savers would be decreased. Thus the people's income might decline two or three times the amount of the impair savings. On the other hand, savings promptly invested to create new capital or wealth would bring full employment and progress, as well as increased demand, for a dollar saved and usefully invested would cause two dollars' worth of demand for consumables.

In the later condensation, *Business Depressions,* he wrote that building activity, expanding auto production, and heavy purchases of foreign bonds would provide the investment opportunities to prevent a slump, but that these fields could not expand indefinitely. During and since the war, he said, United States exports had enormously increased, creating employment for American workers at the expense of workers in other countries. When American capitalists invested their savings in foreign securities, these funds, actually paid to the home producers of the surplus exports goods, had the same effect as savings invested in domestic productive capital. Exports increased business activity and the country became richer, but at the expense of other countries, which through their indebtedness became poorer. When the time should come to adjust the disproportion between exports and imports, when the country's tremendous building activity should settle down to normal, and the auto and radio industries reach the saturation point, this country would be ripe for severe depression.

And the situation would be aggravated should the debtor countries repay their war debts in cash, thus increasing American investment-seeking cash funds.

In his chief treatise, *A Neglected Point,* Johannsen declared that the only solution he could offer was that old, well-developed countries should attempt to have a lower saving propensity than new, progressive countries, and that perhaps the wealthy should purchase more luxuries.[3] But in the same year, 1908, in an article in the *Journal of Commerce,* entitled "How to Relieve the Depression," he offered a more concrete suggestion: that proper financing of the railroads could help bring about a revival. The railroads needed enormous cash funds for development, he said. With a surplus of cash funds in the money market, the roads could not obtain capital, at a reasonable rate of 4 or 4½ per cent, because investors distrusted the roads. This distrust was due in part to the predatory practices of railroad magnates. It could be overcome if a syndicate of bankers, with the power to veto any measure of management, would guarantee the interest on new railroad bond issues, in return for a slight fee. Furthermore, the syndicate could buy up the roads' high-yielding short-term notes, which were, of course, more attractive to investors than 4 per cent long-term bonds. It could obtain funds to buy these notes by following the procedure of stockbrokers who charged their customers 4 per cent on margin accounts and borrowed from the banks on call at 2 per cent. The sellers of the notes, having cash, would naturally be tempted to buy the bonds.

[3] An embryonic version of the doctrine of "impair savings" was presented in a privately printed pamphlet in 1892, called *A Fundamental Principle of Political Economy,* by Edgar J. Rich (1864-1948) who became one of the most prominent lawyers in the country as well as a lecturer at the Graduate School of Business Administration at Harvard. Rich sent a copy to Johannsen in 1926, stating that he had written the essay in 1888 in an effort to meet the reasoning of the classical economists.—Rich to Johannsen, July 19, 1926, letter in possession of Joseph Dorfman.

The expanding roads would create employment, increasing income, and consumption, thereby creating further employment. "And the well-known interplay of activity and reaction, thus started," Johannsen concluded, would help relieve depression. Thus, while in "How to Relieve the Depression" Johannsen approved of increasing bank credit under "extenuating circumstances," he deprecated its use in normal times because it tended to take the form of a permanent investment. In *A Neglected Point* he asserted that only a small part of "bank money" originated from loans made on commercial paper, and that most of it was issued on the security of stocks and mortgages; in other words, banks did not confine their loans to their "legitimate sphere," the discounting of commercial paper, but branched out into the field of permanent investment. True, these loans were not "normally of a permanent nature, being put out on 'call' or on short term." But in reality they constituted permanent investments, for their aggregate did not diminish but expanded, and debtors paid the maturing loans by making new ones, "shifting them from one bank to the other and from one holder of the securities to the other."

Johannsen did not give up his effort to find a cure for depression. While in 1908 he tackled the problem by encouraging investment, in 1913, in his German publication *Die Steuer der Zukunft* ("Taxes of the Future"), he endeavored to meet the problem through discouraging savings and encouraging consumption. He suggested that the government should issue as the circulating medium a paper money which would bear an annual tax of 50 per cent, payable at the rate of 1 per cent a week for the first fifty weeks. Thus, whereas other taxes by reducing purchasing power tended toward a depression, this taxed currency would promote spending. In sending copies of the volume to leading German economists, Johannsen explained that the scheme would stave off the threatening and seemingly inevitable socialist revolution.

Johannsen's scheme was similar to the "stamped money" scheme developed by Silvio Gesell in the nineties, which acquired a certain popularity in America in the thirties and was promoted by Irving Fisher. But there were certain differences in detail between the two plans, especially on the rate of taxation. Furthermore, Gesell meant the scheme to achieve the abolition of rent and interest; but Johannsen, while he contended that his own scheme would lower interest rates, felt that some interest was essential, and he opposed the attack on rent.[4]

In 1920, in *The True Way for Deflation,* Johannsen stated that the inflation was due primarily to the excessive demand for "new constructions, extensions, enterprises," and he suggested that when full employment exists such activities should be restrained. To accomplish this he proposed that in periods of prosperity the Federal Reserve Board be authorized to establish a system of priorities for the granting of private bank credit for large "new undertakings." But the force of his argument was weakened by his insistence that stockmarket speculation continue unhampered, and by his deprecation of any attempts to curtail bank credit for purchases of stock on margin.

On the whole, economists considered Johannsen a crank who did not grasp the ABC of economics. But the exceptions were notable. Elmer H. Youngman, editor of the *Bankers' Magazine,* encouraged him and opened the journal to his writings. John Bates Clark saw merit in Johann-

---

[4] For presentations of Gesell's doctrines, see H. T. N. Gaitskell, "Four Monetary Heretics," in *What Everybody Wants to Know about Money,* edited by G. D. H. Cole (London: Gollancz, 1936), pp. 385-401; Dudley Dillard, "Silvio Gesell's Monetary Theory of Reform," *The American Economic Review,* June 1942, pp. 348-52.

sen's theory that the savings of one class were used to acquire the property of another, and he felt that Johannsen's study of the causes and effects of depressions threw light on the problem. Johannsen's presentation of the mode in which a loss of employment by one group led to loss of employment by another group was also suggestive, Clark thought; although to his mind Johannsen failed to recognize all the limitations of this process of multiplication of the original disaster and overestimated the amount of enforced idleness indirectly caused.[5]

Some of the prominent heterodox economists were more enthusiastic and responsive to Johannsen's ideas. John A. Hobson and Wesley C. Mitchell strongly stressed the merits of his theory in their major works; and the old Fabian Socialist George Bernard Shaw informed Johannsen that the "category of impair savings is a valuable corrective to the ridiculous optimism of our capitalist economists." He hoped that Johannsen would probe deeper into "our frightfully wasteful way of dealing with our capital."[6]

This mixed reception in no way discouraged Johannsen. In the year of his death Johannsen, intellectually vigorous despite his eighty-four years, was still pushing his "specialty, impair savings due to saturation of productive capital," and hoping that after a "long line of disappointments, my endeavors may still reach a successful end."[7]

[5] John Bates Clark, "A New Depression Theory," *The Bankers' Magazine*, February 1909, pp. 256-257.

[6] Hobson, *The Industrial System* (1909; New York: Augustus M. Kelley Publishers, 1969) p. 292; Mitchell, *Business Cycles* (Berkeley: University of California Press, 1913) pp. 18, 19, 389, 569, 580, 581, and *Business Cycles: The Problem and Its Setting* (New York: National Bureau of Economic Research, 1927) p. 25; Shaw to Johannsen, January 2, 1926; letter in possession of Joseph Dorfman. In the 1920's John Maynard Keynes paid respectful attention to Johannsen; see Keynes, *A Treatise on Money* (New York: Harcourt, Brace, 1930) Volume II, p. 100, ft. Friedrich von Hayek then at the University of Vienna was so impressed with Johannsen's 1928 leaflet, *A Depression Manifest*, that he asked for earlier writings; Hayek to Johannsen, April 26, 1928; letter in possession of Joseph Dorfman.

[7] Johannsen to J. W. Martin, March 5, 1928; to Carl Snyder, April 5, 1928, from transcripts from Johannsen's letterbooks.

In reality, they had done so theoretically, for, despite his deficiencies and inconsistencies, there is no question that Johannsen had an acute insight. His general theoretical analysis of saving contains many a germ present in current analyses of economic fluctuations.

A NEGLECTED POINT

IN CONNECTION WITH CRISES

By

N. JOHANNSEN

NEW YORK
THE BANKERS PUBLISHING CO.
1908

INTRODUCTORY

The black central field and the red ring, together, represent the country's money supply; consisting partly of coin, or certificates backed by coin; partly of bank notes; and partly of bank money (deposits in commercial banks, "money in bank").

The black central field represents such of the country's cash funds as are available for investment, or for lending purposes; the red ring, all cash funds not so available and all other money in the country. The lines between the centre and the ring show the movements of money in connection with the processes of saving and investing; the wider the lines, the greater the values they represent.

The Money Market (central field) is fed principally by the red lines, savings, which carry funds from the ring to the centre; it is drained by the black lines, which carry the money back from the centre to the ring. Most of the black lines, but not all of them, represent investments.

The red ring shows, by means of the large arrows, the circulation of money in the regular course of business. It is divided into two sections, pink and carmine. The latter represents the money that happens to be, at a given moment, in the people's possession in the shape of income: money available for expenditures and for buying commodities (Purchase Money). The pink section represents money neither available for

THE INVEST

Showing the Cir

as af

SAVINGS A

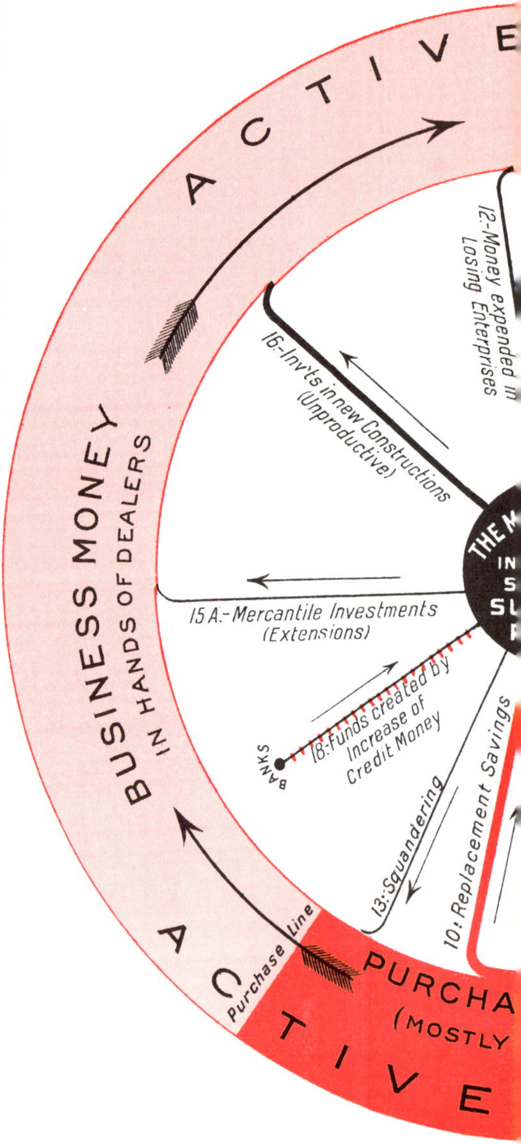

For Expla

NT CHART

tion of Money
d by
VESTMENTS.

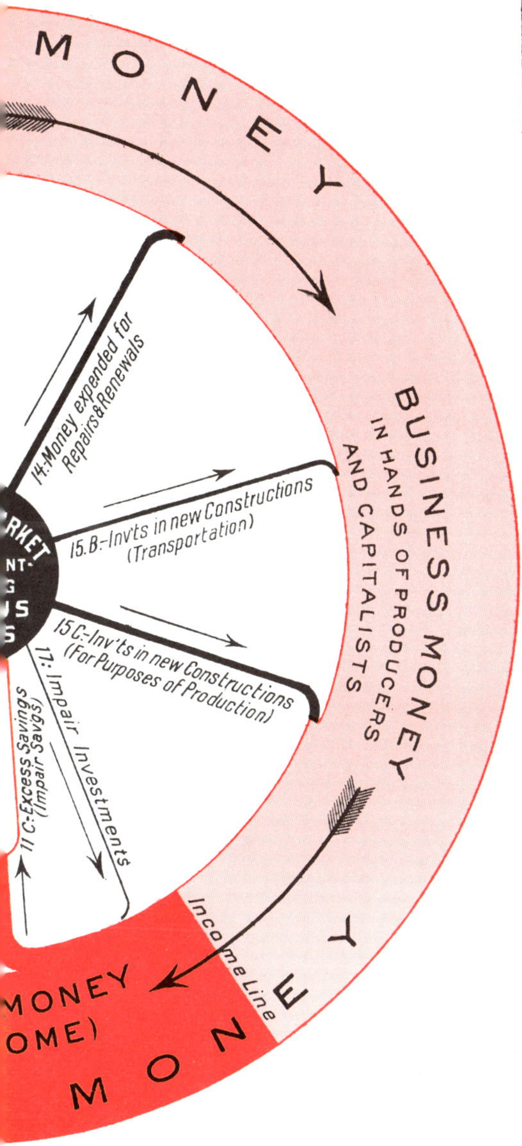

see Page 34.

INTRODUCTORY

CONTINUED

spending nor for investment, being needed by business men for carrying on their regular business.

Whenever "Purchase Money" (Income) is expended in the purchase of commodities, say of a hat costing $2.50, it leaves the carmine field and crosses the "Purchase Line" (which see), becoming Business Money in the hands of the hatter. When he replenishes his stock and new goods are being made, that amount will be split up as follows: the retailer retains $1.00 as his profit; the wholesaler 25c.; the hatmaker 65c.; the manufacturers of the raw material 50c.; the transporters 10c. Thus the Purchase Money, after passing the Purchase Line, will, in its course around the pink circle, reach in turn the retail dealer (lower left), the wholesale dealer (upper left), the manufacturer (upper right), the manufacturer of material (lower right)—each of these parties retaining a portion as income (wages or profits) until the whole of the money in its course around the circle has passed the Income Line (which see) and becomes income again.

The central field is small, compared with the pink field; so are the funds of the Money Market, compared with those employed by business men. It should be well understood that the former are available for investment, but the latter are not; they have already found investment—in the shape of liquid capital needed in business.

DIAGRAMS

SHOWING HOW CERTAIN LINES OF THE CHART ARE AFFECTED BY A CHANGE OF CONDITIONS. FIGURES CONJECTURAL.

Diagram 1. Diagram 2. Diagram 3.

DIAGRAM 1 shows Line 11, with its branches, the same as in the Chart; also Line 17. It is intended to represent the conditions in the United States at a time of great prosperity; for example, such as prevailed in 1900. Practically all of the Net Savings (No. 11), put down at three billions per annum, became useful Capitalistic Savings (No. 11 B), finding employment in Capitalistic Investments (not shown in the diagram). Only a nominal share of the Net Savings became Impair Savings (No. 11 C); these effected their return flow from the Money Market (the black field) in the shape of Impair Investments, represented by Line 17.

DIAGRAM 2 is intended to represent the same lines as diagram 1, as they would appear when affected by a year of depression, such as prevailed in 1894. The Net Savings (No. 11) have fallen from three billions to two billions. And of this amount only one billion (No. 11 B) finds useful employment in Capitalistic Investments, while the other billion represents Impair Savings (No. 11 C), leading to Impair Investments as represented by Line 17.

DIAGRAM 3 is intended to represent these lines in an unprogressive country, like China. The aggregate of Net Savings (No. 11) is but small, and consists almost entirely of Impair Savings (No. 11 C); so the line of Impair Investments, No. 17, is practically equivalent to the line of Net Savings, No. 11. The useful savings, No. 11 C, put down as "nominal," are insignificant, our premise being that the country is unprogressive, and no increase of wealth taking place.

SYNOPSIS.

"Lack of demand" is the characteristic feature of crises and depressions, especially of the latter; lack of demand for working forces[6] as well as for commodities.

The cause of this lack of demand, at times of depression, is practically unknown. Some economists have tried to connect it with the saving process[1]. If a man earns $1,000 and spends only $900, he will create a shortage of demand to the extent of $100, and unless this shortage were counteracted, we would here have a clear case showing how the "lack of demand" is introduced into our economic system as a positive and definite element.

Our economists hold that such counteraction takes place whenever the savings funds[1] come to be invested. In the course of the investment they are finally expended for goods or commodities. Thus, if the said amount of $100 be applied towards building a house and be paid out in the shape of wages to the builders, the latter will expend the money in buying the commodities they need. This constitutes a demand to the extent of $100; not only for goods, but also for such working forces[6] as produce the goods, or, as it were, reproduce them. This demand fully compensates for the original shortage of demand caused by the saving activity—a process which can easily be traced.

But will such compensation also take place where the savings funds find no opportunities to be invested in enterprise and new constructions?[3] At times of depression such opportunities become scarce and the funds have to follow a different mode of investment which is hard to trace. Our economists maintain, that even then a compensation is effected. They point to a very peculiar phenomenon which can always be observed at such times, namely: the savings funds which constantly flow into the money market do not accumulate there (except to a small extent) but find their way back into the channels of production and trade. They cannot get back into these channels without buying goods or commodities in some shape or other. If they do, they create a demand, not only for goods, but also for working forces. The demand thus created by the expenditure of the said $100 will be fully as large as the original shortage of demand ($100) caused by the saving activity.

From these facts, undeniable as they are, our economists have drawn the conclusion that the saving activity cannot result in a real shortage of the demand, provided the savings funds be promptly invested. This conclusion has been universally accepted as correct and has practically become an axiom in modern economics. Still, it is not reliable.

The conclusion loses sight of a certain eventuality. In ordinary business each participant (working-man, trader, capitalist, &c.) furnishes both supply and demand. If A supplies goods or services to the community worth $100 (or draws income from the community in any shape), he subsequently will buy a hundred dollars' worth of goods *from* the community; either he or his family. Just so with B. Ordinarily, therefore, two sets of working forces, A and B, will furnish two supplies and two demands. At times of depression, however, we often find only one supply and one demand between the two sets of working forces, some of the individuals producing without consuming—others consuming without producing, their services being left uncalled for. This leaves part of the working forces without employment and will disturb the equilibrium between the demand for working forces and the supply thereof.

Such unemployment always occurs whenever savings funds are invested in that peculiar manner which characterizes times of depression; the saving process then assuming its "Impairing Form." Exactly how the investment takes place at such times has never been explained by our economists, the subject having escaped their attention. It will be revealed in this present treatise. And it will be shown that, though the savings will finally be turned into goods and commodities, and though this will give employment to working forces, yet unemployment is bound to intervene before this result is reached; unemployment as well as "lack of demand," both due to the saving process.

Once we comprehend the dual nature of the saving process—stimulating business at one time and depressing it at another—we shall not only get a clearer view of the causes underlying depressions but will also know in which direction to look for the remedy.

CONTENTS.

CHAPTER IX.

A NEGLECTED POINT

IN CONNECTION WITH CRISES.

CHAPTER I.

THE APPARENT CAUSE OF CRISES AND DEPRESSIONS.

(The small figures throughout the book refer to Explanatory Notes at the end of the volume.)

MODERN economists make a sharp distinction between crises and depressions, the one designating the shock which marks the end of a reign of prosperity, the other the period of stagnation in trade which follows. In common usage, however, when we speak of a crisis, such a distinction is not made, and a theory purporting to throw new light on the subject is expected not to confine itself to the initial stage, the crisis proper, but to deal largely with the subsequent depression of business—a usage which has been adhered to in selecting the title of this book. In fact, the "neglected point" which I am going to reveal is primarily a factor connected with depressions. At times, however, it has also been the governing factor in developing a crisis.

Despite the common usage of treating crises and depressions as practically one and the same thing, we are justified in distinguishing between the two, for there is a radical difference not only in their outward manifestations but often in their origin. Our economists have hardly gone far enough in this respect. They have dwelt much more upon the difference in the manifestations than upon the difference in the underlying causes. Indeed, the more important crisis theories now extant assume practically one and the same fundamental cause as governing both crises and depressions. Let us see if this assumption can stand scrutiny, and let us inquire into some of these theories in order to ascertain how far the apparent cause of the one will answer to explain the phenomena connected with the other.

The theory most widely accepted holds that a crisis must be attributed to overtrading, too much speculation, extravagance, etc., these various causes absorbing too much of the country's cash capital; and that a period of restriction in enterprise and of retrenchment in expenditures must follow to allow of building up fresh funds of liquid capital. This theory, no doubt, is captivating on account of its simplicity and apparent common sense. It seems plausible that inasmuch as the crisis is marked by a decided money famine, and inasmuch as before the setting in of the crisis there must have been an exhaustion of the country's cash capital, a period of repose and of commercial depression becomes necessary, to permit of recuperation. So it is the dearth of cash funds, occasioned by overtrading, etc., which really would stand as the cause of both—of the crisis as well as of the depression. But do we not here encounter an absurdity? Can the dearth of cash funds be the cause of the depression where as a matter of fact there is no such dearth while the depression exists and where, on the contrary, we witness an excess of idle cash funds? To get around this difficulty the theory had to be enlarged by taking in a new element—the loss of confidence incident to the panic and continuing during the subsequent depression, in consequence of which merchants and manufacturers do not carry on trade and enterprise to the same extent as formerly. This new element, however, does not cover the point either, for confidence is really not lacking and would manifest itself at once wherever an opportunity for a profitable undertaking would offer itself. The fact is, such opportunities are scarce, owing to the prostrate state of trade and the lack of demand; and this lack of demand, which forms the gist of the depression, is neither explained by the loss of confidence nor by the scarcity of cash funds which originally engendered the crisis. The "lack-of-funds" theory, therefore, though fully explaining the setting in of a crisis, and thus accounting for the initial stage of a depression, will not explain why the depression should continue for years in succession. A depression may be *started* by a lack of funds and a loss of confidence; but if it were dependent only upon these two factors, it ought to disappear as soon as these two factors disappear. When the scarcity of cash funds gives place to a plethora, and when the general distrust ceases, the cash funds coming forth from their hiding-places, ready to engage in any promising undertaking, then those two factors which started the depression exist no longer, and the depression itself should cease. And as it does not do so, there must be some other factor at work not covered by said theory.

The latter, therefore, though accounting for the phenomena of a crisis, does not account for the phenomena of the depression.

Another theory, more in accord with the facts, has of late years found many adherents. It hinges on the investment process, and is based on the observation that wherever that process leads to new constructions and to the creation of new productive capital and wealth, the degree of business activity, and therewith of prosperity, bears an almost exact proportion to the extent of such new constructions. Thus, the continuous avalanche of new undertakings and extensions as witnessed in the United States in the years 1905, 1906 and 1907 was coupled with an unprecedented degree of prosperity; ten or twelve years ago, when new enterprises were launched only to a limited extent, business languished; and if we extend our inquiry to unprogressive countries, like China and India, where there are practically no new constructions beyond the replacements necessary to keep up the status quo, we shall find a chronic stagnation of trade accompanied with great poverty of the masses. Wherever we look, we find almost invariably a close proportion between the degree of business activity and the extent of new constructions and enterprises. The funds required for the latter are furnished principally by the saving process—the savings and surplus earnings of individuals all over the country. So long as these savings[1] are invested in new constructions and enterprises, they will give employment and income to the working men and business men engaged in these new constructions, and by means of the well-known process of action and reaction the activity created in these special lines of business will spread to other lines and stimulate demand and activity also among all the numerous trades which are engaged in the broad field of production of commodities—resulting in general business prosperity. But if the savings are not so invested they can not give employment to the working men and business men ordinarily engaged in new constructions, and the lull thus originating in the building lines will react upon general production and trade, and engender a depression.

The foregoing theory, so long as it goes no further than developed above, is undoubtedly correct, and has been accepted by most of our economists, *to that extent.* But the disagreement begins when considering the question, What hinders the savings[1] from continuing to be invested in that beneficent way, i. e., in new constructions[3] and enterprises? Many explanations, differing more or less from each other, have been put forth to answer that question.

Judging this question from my own point of view, I can state two specific causes for the stoppage of new constructions, the one the very opposite of the other: first, The extension of new constructions, like railroads, factories, houses, etc., may have been carried on to such an extent as to satisfy the demand for this kind of capital goods for the time being, thus causing a scarcity of opportunities for investment in this direction; second, the demand for new constructions may become so insatiable as to exhaust the funds of the money market and over-strain the credit facilities of our financial institutions.

The first-mentioned cause became operative with us in 1903 and 1904. In the years immediately preceding, lavish expenditures had been incurred in all sorts of new constructions, or in the extension of old ones, bringing the country's productive power up to a standard much beyond anything previously known, so much so that the demand for productive capital seemed to be satisfied for the time being. In consequence, the pace of new constructions slackened. The trades engaged in new constructions began to suffer, notably the iron and steel trade, and, by means of the well-known process of action and reaction, the dullness in the one line of trade created dullness in most other lines also—all due to the primary cause that the undertaking of new constructions was checked through the abundance of productive capital (railroads, factories, etc.) already in existence.

The second of the two causes above mentioned may seem paradoxical, namely, that an excessive, insatiable demand for new constructions should engender a lull of that demand. But the process is not difficult to understand. An excessive amount of new constructions will absorb an excessive amount of cash capital and will cause a stringency in the money market, so much so that the latter is constantly kept on the verge of a general collapse. If on top of this stringency anything should occur that shakes confidence, all entrepreneurs will take flight at once, and the rush for new constructions will suddenly change to the contrary. If it does, the final result will be the same as in the former case, namely, a lull in new constructions. As soon as this lull sets in, the working forces[6] ordinarily engaged in creating new productive capital and wealth are thrown out of employment, and the loss of income and of buying power on the part of these forces will react upon the forces engaged in the broad lines of production and trade, and engender the depression. Then a new factor sets in. While before the crash the country's productive capital was not large enough to fully meet the great demand for commodities, it is now too large for the reduced demand, so the stimulus for new constructions ceases. Thus we arrive at two factors causing the depression, first, the loss of confidence; second, the shrinkage of the general demand, due to the lull in new constructions. The one factor initiates the depression, the other gives it continuity. The one ceases to operate after the panic is over; the other operates as long as the depression lasts, generally for years in succession. This being so, it is evidently the second factor, the lull in new constructions, which must be considered as the real basis of the depression. And it should be noted that this factor is entirely different from the one which originally gave rise to the crisis.

The foregoing will explain how a stagnation in business may be brought about by either one of two factors, the one the very opposite of the other—a lull in the demand for new constructions on the one hand, and an excessive, insatiable demand for such on the other. In either case we arrive at the same final result, namely, a check to enterprise and to new constructions—the very thing which, according to the view of most economists, forms the governing factor of all depressions.

This view, however, that the degree of business activity largely depends upon the extent of new constructions that happen to be under way for the time being, is not exactly shared in by all of our economists, some of them holding that it looks like putting the cart before the horse. According to their view the demand for new productive capital and for new constructions, such as we witness in seasons of booming business, must be attributed to the great demand for commodities, this being the governing factor; not that the heavy demand for commodities should be brought about by the great extent of new constructions under way. The fact is, we have here a case of reciprocal action. An augmentation in the rate of new constructions brings with it an augmentation of the country's business activity; and an increase in this activity, in turn, will increase the demand for new constructions; the one factor constantly invigorating the other. The governing factor, however, and the one that starts this reciprocal action, must be found in enterprise and new constructions. Suppose a railroad be built in an unprogressive country like China; this will give employment and income to many persons who would otherwise remain idle; these persons, when expending their income for commodities, give employment to other people, those who produce these commodities, and these people in turn, when expending their earnings, will furnish employment to still others, and these again to others, thus giving rise to a chain of action and reaction resulting in an enlargement of the community's total business activity—all of this being due to the building of the railroad.

It seems hardly necessary to adduce further argument to prove how largely prosperity depends upon this important factor: enterprise and new constructions. All experience confirms the fact that wherever the country's savings and surplus earnings are promptly invested in this direction, there business will be active and labor well employed. And experience equally confirms the fact that wherever that all-important factor is dormant, there depression prevails. Such being the case, we are evidently justified in concluding that the theory is correct which holds that the subsidence of enterprise and new constructions, and the causes (whatever they may be) to which the subsidence is due, must constitute the true source of the depression.

This theory seems quite plausible, being sustained by logic as well as by the facts. Nevertheless, it does not cover the ground. It gives only the apparent cause of depressions, not the real one. While we can take it for granted that the presence of the above-named factor, enterprise and new constructions, will stimulate business activity and prosperity, it does not necessarily follow that its absence must entail depression and stagnation in trade.

There is a flaw in the theory. It does not sufficiently consider the question as to what becomes of the country's savings and surplus earnings if they are not invested in enterprises and in the creation of new productive capital and wealth. Why do they, in that case, fail to stimulate trade and prosperity? If they were not invested at all, they would accumulate in the money market, to an immense aggregate, which as we know is not the case. They are evidently invested nearly as fast as they accrue.

And in the course of such investment they return into the channels of general trade, finally becoming scattered in the purchase of commodities. Why does not this sort of investment stimulate prosperity as well?

Let us clearly define the point at issue. If the country's savings and surplus earnings become invested in new constructions, they give employment to a certain class of working forces[6], and business prospers; if invested in a different way, why do they not give employment to some other class of working forces, and why do we see, on the contrary, a general lack of employment? If we could point out the reason why, in the latter case, their investment does not give employment to working forces, might we not fairly hope to obtain new light on the subject of depressions?

Let us follow up this question. We may arrive at conclusions which shall show the existence of a factor, heretofore unknown, that is responsible for the unemployment and the lack of demand prevalent at times of slack business.

The factor considered by many present-day economists as all-important in bringing about a stagnation in trade—the subsidence of enterprise and of new constructions—is only the apparent cause of depressions. A factor more potent than this has escaped their attention. Once we understand the nature of this hidden factor and find means for checking its activity, enterprise and new constructions may practically come to a standstill, and yet business would prosper.

In the foregoing, as well as in what follows, attention has been given primarily to the subject of Depressions, rather than to Crises. The latter are not so difficult to understand, in fact their cause is generally well known, so it would be unprofitable to enlarge upon their discussion. Not so with depressions. Their origin is still so much enveloped in mystery as to justify the conclusion reached above, that there must be factors at work whose existence has heretofore remained unsuspected.

CHAPTER II.

HOW ARE SAVINGS INVESTED AT TIMES OF DEPRESSION?

MOST economists hold that in times of depression the savings and surplus earnings of individuals, then accruing, will largely remain in the money market[4], staying there, for years in succession, in the shape of "liquid capital."

Is this view consistent with the facts? When considering the stupendous annual aggregate of savings made in a country like the United States, the retention of any large portion thereof in the money market would represent a huge sum, entirely out of proportion to the amount of liquid capital actually found there at any one time. When further taking into account that every year of depression ought to increase that huge sum and ought to add to the stock of idle cash funds, while no such increases are revealed by the actual trend of the money market, the above view seems to be quite untenable.

The behavior of the money market, far from showing a growing accumulation of liquid capital at such times, will rather impart the impression that the savings funds flow out about as fast as they flow in, and that a steady absorption of these funds goes on, nearly as fast as at times of prosperous business. True, they are not invested in the field legitimate for savings funds, i. e., in the formation of additional wealth or capital goods, such as railroads, houses, factories, etc., for there is but little of this kind of capital[2] built up in times of depression. But they are surely absorbed in *some* way.

How this absorption is taking place; how those funds

can be invested and transformed into capital[2] without the concurrent creation of new capital—this subject, though of vast practical importance, has not received the attention which it deserves.

* * * * * * * *

Let us, first of all, form an idea of the approximate extent of the country's saving power.

Between the years 1890 and 1900 the wealth of the United States increased about 23 billion dollars, or 2,300 millions per annum. Considering that during the four years of depression from 1893 to 1897 the accumulation went on at a slower rate, the increase must have averaged, for the remaining six years of the decade, as much as three billions. In the recent highly prosperous years, since 1900, it may have averaged not less than four billions.*

Of the latter amount we may safely assume as much as three-fourths to represent savings, i. e., surplus earnings;† and we thus arrive at a total of, say, three billions per annum as approximately representing the country's saving power.

* * * * * * * *

Having thus approximated the saving power, let us see to what extent these savings can find investment in

---

* A recent Government publication states the increase of the country's wealth for the four years 1900 to 1904 to be about 19 billions—almost 5 billions per annum.

† Not all of the country's annual increase of wealth represents surplus income. Part of that increase is the result of appreciation of property, due to a rise in market value; another part may be the result of personal efforts, for instance, where a farmer improves his property by his own toil. If we figure the increase of wealth resulting from these and other sources to be one-fourth of the total increase of four billions, this would leave three billions to represent the wealth derived from surplus income.

All of these figures are guesswork and on that account may not be considered a reliable basis on which to build up an important economic principle. Still, if they are only roughly correct, they answer the purpose of this discussion. Exact figures are neither available nor necessary.

A further discussion of this subject will be found in the footnote on page 115.

the creation of new wealth (i. e., in new constructions) at a time of prosperity and again at a time of depression. It is well known that under prosperous conditions practically *all* of the savings are so invested. Taking this for granted we would arrive at the following equation:

Saving power of the people, per annum................	$3,000,000,000
Savings invested in building up new capital, or in creating additional wealth[3], per annum................	3,000,000,000

Now, suppose a period of depression sets in, equally severe as the one witnessed in the years 1893 to 1897. Our capitalists will not go then into new enterprises to such an extent as they did of late, and will not continue to build up new capital at the rate of three billions a year; perhaps not even at the rate of *one* billion. Assuming the latter amount to be sufficiently near the correct figure, and assuming further that the people's saving power will be reduced by as much as one billion dollars, owing to the depression, our equation would be changed as follows:

Saving power of the people UNDER FAVORABLE CIRCUMSTANCES, per annum, same as above....	$3,000,000,000
Saving power, at a time of depression, reduced to, say	2,000,000,000
Savings actually invested in building up new capital[2], per annum	1,000,000,000

At times of depression only a part of the people's surplus earnings can still be employed in the creation of wealth; according to the above equation only one billion out of two billions of savings. What becomes of the balance?

That balance, whatever it amounts to, is by no means barred from finding profitable investment, and is surely turned into capital[2]. Evidently, if one field of investment becomes closed, another one opens. But how this is done; how savings can be turned into capital without at the same time forming new capital, this question has not so far been treated in a conclusive manner.

A number of theories have been advanced to explain

what becomes of savings funds in times of depression. Let us review these explanations, including the one already referred to, and let us see whether they can stand scrutiny.

EXPLANATION NO. 1.—If savings do not find immediate employment, they will find it later on, after the depression is over; the final investment, such as leads to the formation of new capital, being simply deferred, and the savings meanwhile remaining in the state of "liquid capital." Thus they provide part of the cash funds needed at the time of subsequent recovery in trade. For instance, the savings made during the years of depression from 1893 to 1897, so far as not absorbed *at the time*, constituted part of the cash capital which was utilized later on for the numerous enterprises launched at the time of the ensuing "boom".

REPLY.—If the savings made between 1893 and 1897, or a large part of them, were really left unabsorbed for the time being, *where were they to be found?* Did they stay in the money market?[4] As is well known, savings gravitate toward the latter, appearing there as employment-seeking funds. But even if only one billion dollars per annum, i. e., only one-third of what the savings at the present prosperous time (1907) amount to, had stayed in the money market in the shape of "liquid capital seeking investment," a four years' accumulation would have amounted to four billion dollars of idle cash funds, a sum larger than the whole supply of money in the United States. As a matter of fact, the money market took an entirely different turn. If we take the surplus funds of the commercial banks as a gauge by which to judge the amount of unemployed cash capital extant, we find indeed that a moderate accumulation took place soon after the panic of 1893 had set in, amounting to a few hundred millions; but this accumulation gradually disappeared, so that around 1897 hardly any of it was left—showing that all surplus earnings had been absorbed in the meantime. Do these facts confirm the above "Explanation"?

It may be held that the course which the money market took during those years of depression in the United States was exceptional, and that in other periods of depression the superabundance of liquid capital has been more pronounced. But the principal sign which naturally ought to accompany the steady accumulation of savings funds, viz., the constant growth of unemployed cash funds in the money market, augmenting from year to year while the depression lasts, has never been observed. As a matter of fact the general drift of the money market has not varied much in other depressions, whether in Europe or America, from the course above described. And in none of them has there been an accumulation of funds at all commensurate with the vast amount of savings which flowed into the money market and were not absorbed in new enterprises, and which according to Theory No. 1 should have accumulated there.

Much has been made of the fact that the rate of interest shows a tendency to decline in periods of depression, thus betraying a greater pressure of cash capital to find employment. This pressure no doubt exists; but to deduce therefrom, or from the declining rate of interest, (the cause of which will be explained in a subsequent chapter) that there must be exceptional accumulations of cash funds, although statistics fail to reveal them, is an unwarrantable conclusion. If such idle cash funds, running into billions, really existed, they would first of all appear in the commercial banks. But inasmuch as the weekly bank statistics disprove the existence of these huge idle funds, Theory No. 1 cannot be true.

EXPLANATION NO. 2.—The surplus earnings find *temporary* employment, say in the shape of loans, and in many other ways, until the return of activity in trade ushers in a new demand for liquid capital, and opens up opportunities for permanent investment.

REPLY.—It would not be an easy matter to point out many instances where surplus earnings, or, as it were, the cash funds representing them, find investment of a merely temporary nature. In most instances the supposed temporary investment will either prove to be a permanent one, or will prove to be no investment at all, so far as the funds *as such* are concerned. A real, genuine investment of cash funds will lead them to be split up into hundreds of fragments; they will go in payment for goods or services, will lose the character of cash capital, and will leave the money market. If they do that, they generally have found *permanent* investment. If they do not come to be scattered, they most likely have found no investment at all, but have only changed owners—a subject which will be treated more fully further on. (See "Explanation No. 8.")

Let us analyze a case of what may seem to be a temporary investment. Suppose A saves $1000 and lends the money, for the term of one year, to B, who uses it to extend his factory. When so employed *the money is turned into "fixed capital"* and, though loaned out temporarily only, is permanently invested. By the end of the year B will not be able to return the money, except with the help of *new savings*, or with the help of fresh funds procured elsewhere. He may have saved up that amount of $1000 himself in the meantime; but then the money returned to A represents B's savings, not A's any more; or he may make a new loan elsewhere, and procure the money from C, to pay off A; then the amount represents C's or somebody else's savings. In either case the original funds saved up by A remain permanently invested in the factory.

Just so with the great majority of all other investments, such as may seem to be of a temporary character. Take, for instance, the investment of such funds as are loaned out by the commercial banks of New York to the business community of that city, aggregating more than a billion dollars. Each of those bank loans is of a temporary character, and one should think that the investments for which the funds are used by the borrowers must likewise be of a temporary character. But as a matter of fact, those bank loans represent, *in their entirety*, a permanent investment. The repayment of the individual loans is rendered possible only by the constant issuing of new loans; though not to the same party, still to the community. As soon as the banks try to restrict *the aggregate* of their loans, they meet with great difficulty, for the money needed to repay the maturing loans is not in existence.* That billion dollars, therefore, though seemingly consisting of "liquid capital," turns out to be permanently invested by the business community, and, broadly speaking, no part of it can be re-

* The money is not in existence! This is true, despite the fact that the funds loaned out by the commercial banks are generally redeposited with the banks, and therefore not only in existence but seemingly within their reach. We have to bear in mind that the "money in bank," i. e. the fictitious money represented by bank credits, is the outcome of loans; so, if there is a bank-credit on the one hand there is generally a corresponding loan on the other—and the individuals in whose names the bank credits stand are mostly not those who obtained the loans. Now, if the banks wish to withdraw part of the credit money extant in order to reduce its volume they can not withdraw it from the individuals in whose names the credits stand but must have recourse to those to whom they made the original loans—and since these individuals borrowed the money to invest it in their business, buying either fixed or circulating capital with it, they are no longer in possession of same. These individuals can maintain their solvency only by constant renewals of their loans, eventually shifting them from one bank to the other. But if the banks would try to largely restrict their loans, say by one-half, and would accordingly refuse to make renewals, many of those individuals would simply be unable to pay their maturing obligations, and would have to suspend payments. And the banks would at once find out that the money needed for canceling a large part of their loans, say a quarter or a half of the total, is not in existence. See also footnote on page 23.

turned for good except by the tedious *process of saving* on the part of members of the community.

Outside of the cases here discussed there exist, no doubt, investments of a really temporary character; for instance where a man loans out money to help buying or making season goods, and where the money is returned after the season is over, and after the goods have been sold and paid for. Such transactions would be the only ones that properly come within the scope of "Explanation No. 2". They are quite limited in extent; and, what is more important, they occur oftener at times of great business activity than at times of depression—a fact which economists will hardly dispute. Explanation No. 2 could stand only if such occurrences were much more frequent in hard times, so much so as to employ and absorb a much larger part of the people's savings than is done in times of prosperity. The reverse being true, Explanation No. 2 proves to be utterly inadequate to show what becomes of surplus earnings at times of depression.

EXPLANATION NO. 3.—Periods of great business activity drawn heavily upon the "liquid capital" of the community, so much so as to finally bring about an almost complete exhaustion thereof. The savings made in the subsequent period of depression are needed to replenish the fund of liquid capital available for new enterprises.

REPLY.—The fund of liquid capital can be replenished only by the accumulation of cash funds. As nobody has so far been able to detect the whereabouts of such accumulations, which in the course of a few years of depression ought to run into billions if they were to absorb a large part of the savings, the "replenishing theory" cannot be substantiated. My replies to Explanations Nos. 1 and 2 will also apply here.

The very basis underlying Explanation No. 3 is

wrong, namely, the assumption that for smooth working there should always be a large fund of liquid capital extant, available for new enterprises. Actual facts show this accumulation to be rather small, at active times as well as at dull times. As a rule, savings, the source of that fund, flow into the money market and flow out again, but they do not stay long enough to accumulate to a great extent. That accumulation fund will at no time amount to more than a few hundred millions, so it cannot take billions and billions to replenish it. If, practically, there is no fund to be replenished, the "replenishing theory" cannot stand.

EXPLANATIONS NOS. 4 AND 5.—Before considering these two Explanations individually I will say that both of them refer to the over-straining of credit facilities during the period preceding a depression and to the alleged necessity of a subsequent relaxation. Our discussion of the subject will be helped if we first reach a clear understanding as to *the source* of credit. There are two distinct sources. The one (to be treated in Explanation No. 4) comprises such loans as one individual will make to the other, or as are made by savings banks, life insurance companies, etc., i. e., by such credit institutions as loan out no more money than they receive; the funds originally having accrued from the saving process. The other source (to be treated in Explanation No. 5) comprises loans made by the commercial banks, who create new cash funds of their own, of an artificial nature; bank notes on the one hand and bank credits on the other; the latter being founded on the principle that $1,000 loaned by a commercial bank to an individual is left by this individual on deposit with the bank, or, if transferred by him to other parties, will still remain in the shape of a deposit with some other bank or banks, and will then be used by the business community the same as cash funds ("money in bank") though not really consisting of cash.* Only these artificial cash funds, which have nothing to do with the saving process. come in under Explanation No. 5.

EXPLANATION NO. 4.—At busy times too many enterprises are undertaken "on credit", by incurring debts. The subsequent time of depression and of "forced economy" is needed to pay off at least a part of those debts. During this time the savings of the people are not employed so much towards creating new productive capital as towards cancelling the debit obligations previously contracted.

REPLY.—It may seem quite evident that if people want to pay off their debts, they must save. and that their savings will be absorbed when paying off the debts. But the question arises, What will the receivers of the funds, so paid over, do with them? Are the funds, as such, really absorbed when used for the payment of a debt? Is it not true that they merely change owners and remain "funds available for investment", only in somebody else's hands? If A saves $1,000 and pays this amount to B in cancellation of a debt, B may invest the money in some enterprise, just the same as if it had not previously been used

* This redepositing of the loans constitutes the reason why the deposits in commercial banks represent part of the country's money supply, while those put into savings banks do not. Savings banks, when issuing a loan, part with the money loaned out; the commercial banks do not, broadly speaking. Inasmuch as the funds loaned out by the commercial banks are redeposited with the banks, they practically remain cash funds, and are considered as such and used as such by the business community. Not so with the deposits in savings banks; these represent, not "funds on hand," but "funds invested"; not liquid, but productive capital.

Just so with the Trust Banks. When confining themselves to their legitimate sphere, **they part with the money** deposited with them, and invest it in securities, the same as the savings banks do. The deposits so invested should not be considered as part of the country's money supply.

Of late, however, the Trust Banks have largely gone into the business of commercial banks, not investing their deposits so much in the purchase of securities, but loaning them out, subject to check, the same as commercial banks do. Such deposits, subject to check, should indeed be counted as liquid capital, increasing the country's money supply, and are so counted on pages 154, 156 and 164.

to cancel a debt. Evidently, if B does so invest the funds, the latter did not previously find investment by the act of A paying them over to B; i. e., not by their being used to pay off a debt. Cash funds, *as such*, cannot be considered as having been invested until they are scattered in the general circulation and cease to be "cash funds available for investment", and until they leave the money market. As such is not the case if they are merely used to pay a debt, the theory set forth in Explanation No. 4 to account for the disappearance of savings funds from the money market is not substantiated.*

It is true that at busy times (and in fact at all times) many enterprises are undertaken on credit, one individual borrowing the funds accumulated by another. It is equally true that some of the debts thus incurred by individuals may be cancelled out of savings made by these individuals during the subsequent period of depression. But it is not true that such savings funds should be absorbed and cease to be cash capital when so applied, or should thereby be withdrawn from the money market. If nevertheless they disappear from there, they evidently find an outlet different from the one assigned in Explanation No. 4.

If the assumption were correct that at times of depression the people's savings are more largely applied

* It may seem that we should not only consider the act of paying the debt but also the question as to what the payee does with the money afterwards. Let us take some examples. Suppose he uses it for building a house. If so, the funds would find investment in creating new wealth—while in this chapter we are discussing the question how they can find investment without the creation of new wealth, the fact being that at times of depression (such as we are now considering) the opportunities for the creation of new wealth are quite limited. Suppose he squanders the money. Then an investment does not take place at all, and again we gain no clue as to how surplus earnings are invested in times of depression. This latter point is the only one we are considering in this chapter, and in the text above we are specially considering the question whether the act of repaying a loan constitutes an investment of the money so paid over. We are not discussing the broad question as to what may possibly be done with the money after it has been used for repaying a loan.

toward paying off debts and canceling loans, this tendency should manifest itself in the case of savings banks and insurance companies. The loans they had issued before should be largely paid back to them and they should be at a loss as to what to do with their funds. As a matter of fact, no such tendency manifests itself at times of depression.

EXPLANATION NO. 5.—In periods of great business activity there is more productive capital built up than can be procured from the people's savings accruing at the time; the excess being built up on the strength of funds supplied by credit institutions, with the result of exhausting and unduly straining all credit facilities of the community. The savings made in the subsequent period of depression are needed, therefore, for putting the credit institutions on a sound basis again.

REPLY.—There is some truth in this statement, but very little. As a matter of fact, the credits issued by our financial institutions are not relieved or reduced materially in a period of depression. During our late depression of 1893 to 1897 the credits issued by our commercial banks were reduced by only 135 million dollars. Suppose that this loan reduction was entirely due to the savings made on the part of the borrowers (though it may as well have been due to other causes), could this small amount explain what became of the 4,000 million dollars of savings, which flowed into the money market[4] in the course of those four years, and whose outlet is left unaccounted for?

Let it be well understood that we are dealing here only with such credit institutions as really *create* credit funds, i. e., the commercial banks; not with institutions (like savings banks) who merely lend out funds that were already in existence, and who practically act only as mediators between the owner of such funds on the one hand and the borrower on the other. It is hardly the latter class of institutions which come in consideration when speaking of over-strained credit conditions, for the extent of the credits they grant is bound to keep a close proportion to the extent of the funds entrusted to them by the public. Not so with the commercial banks. With them the amount of credits issued depends largely upon the requirements of the market and a strain may readily take place if they create artificial funds to an extent near the safety limit, either by the issue of bank notes or by the extension of bank credits.

These artificial funds can be used for the creation of new wealth precisely the same as funds accruing from savings. They can be used for that purpose only once,* the same as savings can be used only once. Thus, if their total volume increases from 3 billions to 4 billions, the increase of 1 billion represents cash funds available for building up one billion dollars' worth of new productive capital, or of new commercial capital. At busy times

* It may seem as though such "credit money" can be employed over and over again towards building up new productive capital, inasmuch as it is constantly reverting to the issuers, and constantly being reloaned. But that supposition would be wrong. Most of those reloaning transactions represent a mere shifting of borrowings; a contracting of new debts to pay old ones. Suppose a merchant, A, is short of $50,000 to conduct his business on a cash basis, and that he constantly has notes afloat, aggregating that amount, to make up for the deficiency. These notes, successively issued in payment for the goods he buys, and discounted in various banks, will cause a frequent shifting of cash funds; but the aggregate of these transactions will amount to the same thing as a permanent loan of $50,000 to that merchant, on the part of the banks, as though it were a permanent investment of the banks' credit money in A's business, that bank money having been used by him to build up part of his "circulating capital." Now suppose A saves up $50,000, and pays all his notes, issuing no more of them. Then the banks' funds become free to that amount, to be lent out to some other borrower, B; this time **for real investment purposes**, i. e. for creating new capital goods. But the reader will readily perceive that the funds thus becoming available for investing purposes really consist of A's savings. Seemingly the capital goods created by both A and B, aggregating $100,000, have all been built up with credit money advanced by the banks; but as a matter of fact only $50,000 came from that source, the other $50,000 from the saving process. So the issue of $50,000 credit money will **only once** build up new productive capital to that amount. Every additional million dollars of bank notes or bank loans issued can be made available for creating new wealth to the like amount, **and to that extent only.**

a tendency prevails towards a rapid increase of such "credit money"; at dull times, towards diminishing its volume. To find out how much its volume diminished during our depression of 1893 to 1897, we have to subtract the total volume existing at the end of that period from the total existing before the depression set in; as follows:

Total credit money extant in 1892: Bank notes $174; loans of National Banks $2171; of State Banks $757 millions; in all..................................	$3,102,000,000
Total credit money extant in 1897: $230; $2067; $670 millions; in all...	2,967,000,000
Showing a decrease of..................................	135,000,000

This small reduction of 135 millions* can, at best, account for the absorption of only *an equal amount* of the savings made during that period; but does not explain what became of the balance of the savings. If, as assumed in the early part of this chapter, the total of the savings, left unaccounted for, amounted to 1000 millions per annum, or 4000 millions for the four years from 1893 to 1897, the small share of this total which is represented by the above-stated amount of 135 millions cuts no figure.

* * * * * * * *

The importance of credit money, in so far as it contributes cash funds towards building up new productive capital, seems to have been much exaggerated by our economists. That amount is quite small, when compared with the amount supplied by the saving process. Savings funds are always flowing into the money market quite freely; but they soon find investment and disappear, never to be seen again, while credit money will constantly reappear in the money market and be lent out over and

* The deposits in Trust Banks are not considered in the above statement. At that period the Trust Banks did very little business of such character as the commercial banks do (see footnote, page 20), so their deposits could not, at that time, be classed the same as deposits in commercial banks and did not really constitute part of the country's money supply.

over again, a fact which may impart the impression that there is more productive capital built up with credit money than with savings funds. We should bear in mind, however, that credit money can be used for that purpose only once, *and only in proportion as its total volume increases.* The following figures will serve to show the extent of this increase, for the years 1890 to 1900:

1890: Total of credit money then extant: Bank notes $186; loans of National Banks $1986; of State Banks $581 millions; in all	$2,753,000,000
1900: $310; $2710; $1030 millions; in all	4,050,000,000
Showing an increase of	1,297,000,000

Was the whole of this latter amount available for new constructions, or the creation of new wealth? Hardly. Part of it was tied up owing to the fact that the banks needed so much more legal reserve; another part was absorbed by losing enterprises, by squandering, by repairs, replacements, etc. For the sake of argument let us assume that out of the $1,297,000,000 increase of credit money just stated, as much as one billion was available for new constructions, though in reality it was less. During the same period of 1890 to 1900 the country's wealth increased by about 23 billions. Of this amount perhaps one-quarter was made up by "appreciation of value" (see footnote, page 12), the balance, say 15 billions, by the creation of new wealth. Of the cash funds necessary to create this wealth there was one billion supplied by the issue of credit money, the balance, say 14 billlions, by the saving process.

Reviewing explanation No. 5 in the light of these figures, we find that only a small share of the productive capital (in this case one-fifteenth) is being built up with credit money; and of this small share only a small part is cancelled in a period of depression—only 135 millions during the said four years. Were the reverse true; were the cash funds required for new enterprises supplied principally by the issue of credit money, and were a large proportion of this credit money cancelled by the savings made during a subsequent depression, then we could argue that there is an inherent necessity for a period of depression to follow a period of strained credits and of great business activity. Then, Explanation No. 5 would stand substantiated. But not where all facts point to the contrary.*

EXPLANATION NO. 6.—The surplus funds are to a larger extent absorbed in "unproductive consumption," which results in an increase of the demand.

REPLY.—This argument is met quite often in modern economics. On general principles it may seem obvious that if on the one hand the surplus earnings are not applied toward new constructions or the creation of new wealth, and on the other they do not accumulate in the money market, they must be used, to a greater extent than usually, for the purpose of consumption. In fact, many economists share in the belief that if towards the end of a boom period it appears that more productive capital has been built up than the demand for the time being will warrant, and if in consequence a tendency arises to abstain from new constructions, then the surplus earnings, finding only partial employment in new constructions, are more largely applied towards the satisfaction of personal wants—for the purchase of luxuries and consumptibles. And the theory has it that as a result of this increased purchasing power, which means an in-

* In the foregoing the fact that, from 1893 to 1897, an amount of $135,000,000 of loans was repaid to the financial institutions, has been attributed to the assumption that this amount represented so much savings, but, as already stated, this reduction of the loan account may be due to other causes; for instance, to the shifting of loans from the commercial banks to the trust companies, or to the reduced demand for accommodation on the part of business men, consequent upon the lessened activity of trade. If so, there would not remain even a nominal basis for Explanation No. 5.

creased demand for consumptibles, and naturally an increased production of the latter, the general demand prevailing in the country will·expand and gradually become large enough to fully employ the productive capital then in existence, whereupon a demand for additional productive capital will spring up and usher in a new boom period.

According to this theory the demand for consumptibles is greater in a depression period than in a boom period—a conclusion which runs counter to all experience.

Again, if people, instead of accumulating and investing part of their income, will spend it in luxuries (which is the gist of the above theory) we cannot talk of "surplus earnings" any more; the latter representing such income as is left after providing not only for the necessaries of life but also for luxuries.

If there is more "unproductive consumption" at times of depression, and if such unproductive consumption will afford opportunities for real investment of surplus earnings, the modus operandi should be explained. That has not been done so far. Explanation No. 6, therefore, neither explains what becomes of surplus earnings at such times, nor does it agree with the facts when assuming that they are employed towards increasing the demand for consumptibles. Times of depression do not show an increase of consumption.

EXPLANATION NO. 7.—The surplus funds are applied in a larger measure for unproductive public expenditures, for the building up of what we may call "unproductive capital"; such as schools, works of art, embellishment of cities, sanitary improvements, hospitals, etc.

REPLY.—This assumption likewise runs counter to actual facts. In years of depression the expenditures made for such purposes do not increase; on the contrary, they decline.

This is still more true of *private* expenditures for unproductive purposes, such as the buying of carriages, automobiles, yachts, palaces, pictures, etc. Nobody will dispute that less money is spent on such investments in hard times, even by the rich. Point No. 7 would hold good only if the reverse were true, i. e., if *an increased* amount were spent at such times.

EXPLANATION NO. 8.—The surplus funds are more largely absorbed by investments in mortgages and public securities

REPLY.—Many people think that the mere purchase of bonds and mortgages, already issued and already in the market, constitutes an investment. It does so from the standpoint of the individual capitalist, but not from that of the cash funds as such. If A buys a bond from B for $1000, the purchase will no doubt constitute an investment so far as A personally is concerned; but the money *as such* does not find investment by the purchase; it continues to be idle, investment-seeking cash capital, only in B's hands instead of A's. And it remains in the money market, now as before. What B does with the money *later on* has nothing to do with our subject, and in this connection I refer to the foot-note on page 21; what has been said there will also apply here. So we are justified in saying that the mere purchase of bonds or mortgages, where the purchase money remains in the shape of cash capital, does not constitute a real and final investment for cash funds, and cannot possibly form an outlet for the savings funds which keep on flowing into the money market and which nevertheless do not accumulate there.

EXPLANATION NO. 9.—The surplus earnings find investment *abroad.*

REPLY.—In what shape do they go abroad? In the shape of money? Or of merchandise? Or through the instrumentality of foreign exchange?

Most people believe that funds can be sent abroad without the necessity of gold shipments; say, by bankers' drafts; i. e., by a mere shifting of credits. But this is not so. Very few people have a clear conception of the function of foreign exchange, and the less they know about it the more are they inclined to attribute all sorts of mysterious powers to its agency. A discussion of this subject will be found in the footnote on page 116.

As to the migration of surplus earnings in the shape of cash, statistics do not bear out the idea that during hard times billions of money are sent abroad. This would necessitate large remittances of gold, while as a matter of fact a country's net movement of gold (the "net" being the difference between a year's exports and a year's imports) is not seriously affected by a period of depression, and the balance may as well appear on the credit side as on the debit side. As a rule such shipments of gold merely represent the residual balances of foreign trade transactions, very seldom foreign investments. And invariably they are of a rather limited extent.

Nor do statistics bear out the idea that in hard times the surplus earnings go abroad in the shape of merchandise. This would necessitate a sudden enormous increase of exports without a corresponding increase of imports. True, there is a reason why exports should expand at such times, inasmuch as wages and prices shrink, and the home market thus becomes better fitted to meet foreign prices and to enter into foreign competition. But such an expansion of the exports is a plant of slow growth and really depends upon commercial causes and market conditions, not upon the intention of capitalists to invest their funds abroad. Under favorable market conditions such increase of exports takes place anyway. If it does, and if in consequence a country's foreign trade leaves a balance in its favor, showing a surplus of, say, $100,-000,000, then the capitalists of that country may invest this amount in foreign securities, instead of having that balance paid over in the shape of cash; and there we would have a clear case of investing capital "abroad". The rule is, however, that there must first be a favorable trade balance and then there is room for investing domestic funds in foreign securities—a subject which will be more fully discussed on page 134. To assume that at times of depression capitalists will buy up large lots of domestic goods, and send them to foreign countries, in addition to the usual movement of export goods—this idea is not worth serious consideration and is in no way borne out by statistics.

We have to conclude, therefore, that at such times our idle surplus earnings cannot find employment by migrating abroad.

EXPLANATION NO. 10.—In times of depression the saving power of the community relaxes, resulting in a shrinkage of the volume of savings and surplus earnings, and therewith of the funds which constantly flow into the money market to seek investment there. Thus, if on the one hand there are admittedly less opportunities for investment, there are, on the other hand, *less funds looking for investment.*

REPLY.—This view is undoubtedly correct. Inasmuch as the earnings of the people fall off, their saving power as well as their aggregate savings will decrease. But that does not do away with the fact that of the savings still remaining only a part is being absorbed by new constructions—a fact which economists will hardly dispute. To bring this point out more clearly, let us illustrate it by the use of figures.

Let us assume that:

The aggregate surplus earnings per annum in prosperous times (practically all of them being invested in the creation of new capital[2] or wealth) come to....	$3,000,000,000
At a time of depression the aggregate annual surplus earnings shrink to	2,000,000,000
Of which amount there is invested in the creation of new wealth[3], say....................................	1,000,000,000
Leaving a balance of surplus earnings, the mode of investment of which is not known, amounting to....	1,000,000,000

Whether the last-mentioned figure should be one billion, or only half a billion, does not matter much for the sake of our argument. It certainly is a large amount. And the disappearance of this large share of the savings is left unexplained by Explanation No. 10. The latter only states that the total of the savings will fall off; but it does not show what becomes of the savings that are still being made. To show that, is just the point in question.

Explanation No. 10 would cover the point only if the aggregate savings could be assumed to diminish always at the same rate as the opportunities for building up new capital[2] diminish; as it were, that a million dollars of savings could be made only if there were opportunities for investing that amount in the creation of new wealth, and that if there were no opportunities for investing more than half a million in that manner, no more than the latter amount could be saved. Such an assumption, however, could neither be proved by theory nor substantiated by facts.

In the foregoing pages I have reviewed the various explanations now extant purporting to show how surplus earnings are invested in times of depression, and I have proved every one of these explanations to be untenable. While it is generally conceded that at such times the surplus earnings do not find investment in new constructions (except to a limited extent) the true manner of their investment has never been revealed. I have demonstrated that:

First.—They do not accumulate in the money market.

Second.—They do not, to a larger extent, go into investments of a temporary character.

Third.—They do not assume the shape of "liquid capital."

Fourth.—They do not become absorbed when used for paying debts.

Fifth.—They are absorbed only to a very limited extent, if at all, in augmenting the reserves of the credit institutions.

Sixth.—They are not dissipated in luxuries, or in a greater satisfaction of personal wants.

Seventh.—They are not, in a larger measure, applied to the creation of what we might call "unproductive capital."

Eighth.—They do not become absorbed if invested in the mere purchase of mortgages, securities, etc.

Ninth.—They do not go abroad to find investment there.

Tenth.—The theory that the aggregate of savings diminishes in the same proportion as the opportunities diminish for investing them in new constructions or in the creation of additional wealth, cannot be substantiated.

* * * * * * * *

No doubt a shrinkage in the aggregate of savings or surplus earnings takes place, when times of depression set in. Nevertheless it is generally conceded that at such times large volumes of savings funds would still be available for new enterprises if there were opportunities for profitable investment in that direction. These savings funds keep on right along flowing into the money market;

only part of them is absorbed in the creation of new wealth; the balance disappears; but the nature of the outlet still remains to be discovered. Where does that balance go?

That question, though seemingly of a purely academic character, is of vast practical importance. If we can answer it, we may find ourselves in possession of the key to the solution of the greatest problem of the age: the cause of depressions.

CHAPTER III.

THE INVESTMENT OF SAVINGS AT TIMES OF DEPRESSION.

EXPLANATION OF THE CHART.

BEFORE inquiring into the nature of the peculiar class of investments mentioned in the title of this chapter, let us broadly define what constitutes an investment as such, and what changes cash funds have to undergo before they become invested.

To this end let us conceive the country's money supply to be divided into two classes: "Active Money" on the one hand, as represented by the Red Ring of the Chart, and "Surplus Funds" on the other, the latter constituting the "Money Market," the central field of the Chart.

The first class, Active Money, comprises by far the greatest part of the money wealth, viz., all that is employed in industry and trade, wage funds, people's earnings so far as intended to be expended for consumptibles, and all funds held by business men for purposes of regular current business.*

The second class, Surplus Funds, comprises such funds as are not engaged in carrying on regular current business, but are idle, and available for investment. These funds originate principally from the surplus earnings of the savers (represented in the Chart by the red savings lines 10 and 11, which build up the central field);

* Such funds may be temporarily idle; but inasmuch as the owner cannot afford to invest them elsewhere, and will sooner or later need them again for his regular business, they belong in the class of Active Money, i. e., in the red ring of the Chart.

to a small extent also from the increase of artificial money issued by the commercial banks, such as bank notes and bank credits; which increase is represented in the Chart by the red-and-black line No. 18.

We should keep this distinction between Surplus Funds (black central field) and Active Money (red ring) well before us in order to answer the above-stated question as to what constitutes an investment. The latter necessitates ***the transformation of Surplus Funds into Active Money.***

While the act of saving generally withdraws Active Money from the channels of industry and trade and turns it into the Money Market, the act of investment will turn it back from the Money Market into the channels of industry and trade. In terms of the Chart: while the red savings lines emanating from the "Income Field" transmit cash from the ring to the centre, transforming it from "Active Money" into "Surplus Funds," the black investment lines emanating from the central field carry it back from there to the ring—from the unproductive circulation of the Money Market into the productive circulation of industry and trade. They transform "Surplus Funds" into "Active Money."

This transformation constitutes a vital condition of an investment. Surplus Funds, in order to be invested, must cease to be "funds available for investment." Merely changing the ownership of such funds does not invest them; for instance, in buying a house. But *the building* of a house does. A thousand dollars, if spent in building or creating any kind of property, will be scattered into many hands, will generally be turned into income for the direct or indirect receivers, and will cease to be cash capital. This scattering of the compact money mass—the return of the money into the channels of industry and trade for purposes of production or consumption—that is what constitutes the essential feature of an investment. Without this scattering of the cash funds no investment takes place.

* * * * * * * *

Of such investment lines our Chart shows quite a number, each one denoting a separate and distinct class of investment. Of the red savings lines, which emanate from the "Income Field," the Chart shows only two, "Replacement Savings" and "Net Savings," the distinction between these two classes being based on the manner of investment—whether the savings are available for increasing the country's wealth and for creating new productive capital, or whether they are absorbed in merely keeping up the standard of the capital already in existence and in making up for deterioration and losses. In other words, the distinction as to whether they must be classed as Replacement Savings or as Net Savings depends upon the outlet from the Money Market, whether they find it by means of Lines 12, 13 and 14, or by means of Lines 15, 16 and 17.

LINE No. 10 represents "Replacement Savings," i. e., such savings as are absorbed in maintaining the standard and efficiency of existing capital, property, or wealth. The manner of their absorption is shown by the investment lines 12, 13 and 14. Line No. 12 stands for "Losing Enterprises," where cash capital is sunk in injudicious or fruitless undertakings; the accumulation of such cash capital (or eventually the subsequent replacement of it) evidently absorbing savings. Line No. 13 stands for "squandering"; a spendthrift may sell his house and squander the proceeds, while the man who supplies the money and takes the house for it, finds investment for his savings. Inasmuch as the spendthrift expends his money for consumptibles, he transforms "Surplus Funds," the savings of others, into "Purchase Money," a process which can be followed on the Chart. Line No. 14 stands for "Repairs and Renewals," such as are necessitated in consequence of wear and tear, the ravages of time, accidents, conflagrations, floods, storms, etc.

It is plain that out of the total of savings accruing, a certain part is required to make good the losses resulting from the causes enumerated above; and this part of the savings is represented separately in the Chart, by the red line No. 10—Replacement Savings.

LINE No. 11 represents "Net Savings"; i. e., such savings as are not absorbed by any of the factors just alluded to, and which are therefore available for new constructions and for the augmentation of wealth. The manner of their absorption is shown by the investment lines 15A, 15B, 15C, 16 and 17.

As will be noticed, Line No. 11 divides into two branches, one of them being designated as "No. 11 B, Capitalistic Savings," the other as "No. 11 C, Excess Savings," this distinction indicating the difference in the final results whch the savings lead to. The fact is that while all "Net Savings," as represented by Line No. 11, are available for the augmentation of the country's wealth, only a part of them really comes to be employed for that purpose, which part is represented by the branch of Line No. 11 designated as "Capitalistic Savings;" while the other part, designated as "Excess Savings," is not so employed. The mode of investment of these two sub-divisions of "Net Savings," therefore, is quite different, which difference can be traced in the Chart, as follows:

"CAPITALISTIC" SAVINGS (No. 11 B) are, as stated, those which lead to the creation of new capital[2] or wealth, finding their avenues of investment through the lines 15 A, 15 B, 15 C and 16. Line 15 A stands for cash funds moving into mercantile enterprises, increasing the "circulating capital" by opening new commercial establishments and extending old ones. Line 15 B stands for cash funds which are being employed in the extension of transportation facilities, such as railroads, ships, roads, canals, etc. Line 15 C stands for cash funds in course of conversion into new productive enterprises, especially manufacturing, mining, and agriculture; also tenement houses, etc. Line 16 stands for cash funds being invested in what may be termed "non-productive capital," such as hospitals, public schools, municipal buildings, parks, houses occupied by the owners, pictures, libraries, etc.

"EXCESS" SAVINGS (Line 11 C) constitute that part of the "Net Savings" which, though available for new enterprises, or for the creation of new wealth, do not find an outlet in that direction. Their avenue of investment is represented in the Chart by Line No. 17, "Impair Investments." Their peculiar manner of investment has never been explained so far, and will be the subject of the present chapter.

On the last page of the Chart will be found Diagrams 1, 2 and 3, the purport of which is fully covered by the accompanying text. These diagrams will be referred to in this treatise as occasion demands.

IMPAIR INVESTMENTS.

Savings[1] generally flow to the money market, where they seek investment—a process which has been illustrated by the red lines of our Chart. These savings, so far as they are not absorbed for "Replacement" purposes, are available for the creation of new capital or wealth. In times of depression, however, this, their natural field of investment, becomes quite limited, and will no longer absorb all the funds available for that purpose. Then a part of these funds is left over. The part thus remaining has been designated in the foregoing pages as "Excess Savings."

These Excess Savings should be expected to accumulate in the money market; as a matter of fact, however, they do not. They evidently find some outlet from there, almost as readily as if absorbed in new enterprises. How this is done, nobody knows. They are, no doubt, turned into capital[2], but a corresponding creation of new capital does not take place.

The explanations so far given by our economists to account for this strange phenomenon have proved to be untenable—a conclusion which has been fully demonstrated in the previous chapter.

* * * * * * * *

To present the subject at issue in a form more readily understood, let us resort to figures, and to this end reproduce the equations given on page 13, which show how savings are affected and investments changed in their character by the recurring seasons of prosperity and depression. The changes thus brought about can also be followed up in Diagrams 1 and 2, *which see.*

MANNER OF INVESTING SAVINGS AT A TIME OF PROSPERITY.

(See Diagram 1)

	Dollars
Annual savings available for the creation of new capital[2] (the "Net Savings" of the Chart).....................	3 billions
Savings actually invested in new constructions[3] (the "Capitalistic Savings" of the Chart) nearly..........	3 billions
Savings left over (the "Excess Savings" of the Chart)..	Nominal

MANNER OF INVESTING AT A TIME OF DEPRESSION.

(See Diagram 2)

	Dollars
Annual savings available for the creation of new capital (Net Savings), as assumed on page 13,—the saving power of the people having been cut down by one billion, owing to a diminution of income.............	2 billions
Of which amount only a part is actually invested in new constructions (said part representing the Capitalistic Savings), say	1 billion
Leaving an amount of "Excess Savings," the mode of investment of which is not known, of.................	1 billion

Whether this last figure, representing the "Excess Savings," should be exactly one billion, or a different amount, does not matter. In any event the amount of savings not invested in the creation of new wealth is quite large at times of depression—a fact which economists will hardly dispute.

From the above figures, rough as they are, a conclusion can be drawn which will throw a peculiar light on the mode of investment of the funds in question. Inasmuch as the saving process enriches the savers, increasing their aggregate wealth by two billion dollars, and inasmuch as the aggregate wealth of the country as a whole increases only by one billion, the acquisition of wealth on the part of the savers must be accompanied by impoverishment[9] on the part of other members of the community. In other words: If Net Savings are not invested so as to augment the country's wealth or capital, and if they find their final investment in some *other* way, they will, though benefiting the saver, do so only at the expense of "others." The savers will become richer; "others" poorer.

To render this point still more clear, let us again resort to figures. Let us assume the wealth of the country to amount to 100 billion dollars, of which one half is owned by the savers, the other half by non-savers; and let us ascertain how the holdings of the latter class (which class, by the way, represents the great mass of the people) are affected by the saving process in a year of prosperity and how they are affected in a year of depression.

CHANGES OF WEALTH IN A YEAR OF PROSPERITY.

		Dollars
Jan. 1st.	Property held by the savers	50 billions
	Property held by the non-savers	50 billions
	Total holdings	100 billions
Dec. 31st.	Total holdings, the saving process having added 3 billions of new capital	103 billions
	Of which amount the savers own	53 billions
	Leaving for the non-savers, the same as at the beginning of the year	50 billions

CHANGES OF WEALTH IN A YEAR OF DEPRESSION.

		Dollars
Jan. 1st.	Total holdings, same starting figures as above, aggregating	100 billions

Dec. 31st.	Total holdings—only one billion of savings, out of a total of two billions, having been used for building up new constructions............	101 billions
	Of which amount the savers own, having augmented their holdings by two billions........	52 billions
	Leaving for the non-savers, instead of 50 billions as at the beginning of the year, only..	49 billions

Here the non-savers, representing the bulk of the community, have become poorer by one billion as a sequel to the fact that savings to that amount, made by others, failed to be invested in the creation of new wealth,* but were invested in some other way. Granting the fact that at times of depression there are more savings made than can, for the time being, find investment towards increasing the community's wealth, it follows with certainty, from the above calculation, that the body of non-savers must become poorer to the full extent of the savings not so employed; i. e., to the full amount of the "Excess Savings."

A great deal, therefore, depends upon the manner of investment, as to whether it leads to the creation of new wealth, or not. In the one case the community is benefited; in the other, a part of it suffers a certain impoverishment.[9] To distinguish these two kinds of invest-

* The above calculation, which forms the basis of my saving-theory, will, in the subsequent parts of this treatise, be referred to as the "Basic Calculation."

To economists this calculation may, at first sight, seem to be erroneous, and the impression may prevail that if the savers become richer by 2 billions, the community must also become richer by that much. That this does not necessarily follow, is proved, however, by the well known squandering process. The spendthrift who sells his house and spends the proceeds, becomes poorer; the saver who supplies him with the money and takes the house for it, becomes richer. So the enrichment of the latter is offset by the impoverishment[9] of somebody else, and is not accompanied by an increase in the aggregate wealth of the community. The savings are invested, but without the creation of new capital[2].

Just so in the case covered by our calculation: the investment of the one billion of "Excess Savings" does not augment the wealth of the community, but hinges on the acquisition, by the savers or their representatives, of property already existing, in connection with the impoverishment of its previous owner.

The causes of the impoverishment[9] are radically different, however, in the two cases here cited. It is brought about by the voluntary doings of the individual in the one instance, and in the other by general market conditions entirely beyond the individual's control.

ment, let us designate the one as "Capitalistic (i. e. capital-producing) Investments," linking with the "Capitalistic Savings" spoken of on page 37, the other as "Impair Investments"[8]—the latter term having been used on page 38, as well as in the Chart. Of these two forms of investment the first one is well known to the reader and needs no discussion; so we may confine ourselves to the investigation of the second, the "Impairing Form of Investment" (i. e., the investment of Excess Savings), and above all enquire into the nature of the impoverishment caused by it. To this end I shall take up three questions which naturally present themselves in connection with the subject, viz.:

1st. Is the impoverishment,[9] as evinced by the aforesaid "Basic Calculation," merely a matter of calculation based on assumed figures, or is it proved by actual facts?

2d. If a matter of fact, how is it brought about? What is the modus operandi?

3rd. What has the impoverishment[9] of the community to do with the investment of "Excess Savings"?

Let us take up each of these questions separately.

* * * * * * * *

QUESTION NO. 1.—*Is there much impoverishment*[9] *going on among the people at a time of depression?*

There certainly is. In fact, that is one of the principal features of a depression. Anywhere and everywhere we meet people who complain of reduced earnings, of poor business, of their inability to make both ends meet. All over we find men out of employment, or working only part of the time, and struggling hard to procure even the most urgent necessaries of life—business men running behind, and property-owners being compelled to encumber their holdings. Wherever people do not enjoy a fixed income; wherever their earnings depend upon the course of business; and wherever they do not belong to the favored few who are well to do and who still can save and accumulate, there we find wealth waning and poverty spreading.

The "Basic Calculation," therefore, agrees with the facts. And in turn, the facts prove the correctness of our calculation—at least so far as the underlying principle is concerned.

* * * * * * * *

QUESTION NO. 2.—*How is this impoverishment*[9] *brought about?*

We can readily trace the cause when considering the fact that at times of depression but little new capital[2] is being built up and that most of the "working forces"[6] ordinarily engaged in new constructions are thrown out of employment. These "Constructive" Forces comprise not only the workmen immediately concerned, but also manufacturers, contractors, dealers, the men engaged in transportation and in the production of raw material, etc., all of whom find their income either stopped or reduced and accordingly become poorer. Let us designate these people in their entirety as "Class C"*.

As soon as Class C commences to suffer from the impoverishment process caused by the lull in new constructions, a new element of disturbance, which we will call the "Multiplying Principle," comes into play, aggravating the harmful effect. The impoverishment is not confined to Class C, i. e. to the Constructive Forces,[7] but will spread further. The individuals constituting that class, finding their income stopped or reduced, have to reduce their expenses accordingly. They will buy less of

* The individual members of class C, or any other class, are affected to a very uneven extent; the one member, a workingman, may lose all of his income; another member, a merchant, only a small part of it. A merchant may be a member of each of a good many classes.

commodities than before. In consequence of that, the producers and distributers of such commodities as class C had been buying, will likewise be affected, the demand for these goods falling off. Withal *the production* of these commodities will be reduced; and, as a further sequence, *the earnings* of the producers will decline. So the harmful effect is not limited to the members of class C, the Constructive Forces, but will extend further, multiply as it were, and reach those engaged in the production of commodities, i. e. the "Commodity Working Forces."[7]

To illustrate this matter by an example, let us single out ten working men, forming part of class C, and assume that, when employed, their aggregate earnings amount to $5,000 per annum. They spend that money in the purchase of commodities. When these commodities are produced anew, that money will become income for those who are engaged in reproducing them. Let us designate these producers (including the distributers), *so far as they are directly affected by the purchases of those ten men*, as "Class D." When the members of class D, in turn, expend their earnings, that same money becomes income for class E, and so on for classes F, G, etc., the succession of income and expenditure forming practically an endless chain. Now cut off the income of those ten men in class C, and the whole chain will be affected. The expenditures of class C may be reduced from $5,000 to $1,000,* thus diminishing the income of class D by

* The members of class C surely do not reduce their expenditures **to nothing**, for they do not exactly **starve** with their families and are not left without food and clothing and shelter, but will manage, by hook or crook, to obtain the most urgent necessaries of life. If they have an account at the sevings bank, they will draw against it. If they have furniture which they can spare, or other kind of property they can dispose of, they will sell it. They will leave the rent unpaid, and thus pirate on the landlord; or they may pirate on their friends, by borrowing from them. Eventually they will appeal to the charity of others. On the whole, our assumption that if they lose their regular income of $5,000, they still will expend $1,000, may not be far from the truth.

$4,000; which means a total loss of income of $9,000 to the two classes combined. The income of class E may decline to the extent of $2,000 or $3,000, which brings the total loss up to $11,000 or $12,000. This total will keep on swelling as the harmful effect spreads further. True, for each successive link of the chain the loss becomes smaller, being divided up, at the same time, among a greater number of individuals.* Still, the losses are there, and, whether light or heavy, they are felt by all classes affected, and in their aggregate represent a much larger amount than the original loss of $5,000 which befell class C. Here we have an illustration of the modus operandi of the "Multiplying Principle."

To form an estimate of the extent to which the income of the community at large can be affected by the factors here discussed, we must recall the figures given in the early part of this chapter. Let us retain the assumption that while during the prosperous period of 1907 the total surplus earnings of the people amounted to 3 billion dollars per annum and were fully absorbed in the creation of new wealth, the amount shrank to 2 billions after the depression set in, out of which sum only 1 billion is being absorbed in the creation of new wealth, instead of 3 billions as before. Then two-thirds of the "Constructive Working Forces,"[7] i. e. two-thirds of the individuals constituting class C, will be put to idleness, and will lose income to the amount of 2 billion dollars per annum. This loss of income on the part of class C will entail a loss of income on the part of class D, of probably not less than one and a half billion. The loss to class E will be less than that, and still less will be the respective losses to classes F, G, etc. If we put down

* If class C counts 10 members, class D (i. e. those who are directly affected by the purchases of class C and derive income therefrom) may count 1,000 members; class E (those who derive income from the purchases of class D) 5,000 members, class F 10,000, and so on.

another billion and a half as the aggregate loss of all the other groups, a figure which may not be too high, the grand total of the annihilation of earnings would be brought up to 5 billion dollars per annum. If we compare this sum with the amount of the aggregate actual earnings, which has been computed at over 20 billions per annum, we find that one-fourth of the former income of the people may thus be annihilated. This would be the outcome if earnings to the amount of one billion dollars were invested in the "Impairing Form"[8]; i. e., if they did not lead to the creation of new wealth.

The above-stated proportion of one-fourth may seem excessive. Whether the annihilation of income be put down as a fourth, or only as a fifth, or a sixth of the total, does not matter much. My object is not to establish exact proportions, but to bring out the general principle and to show that an interruption in the process of building up new capital[2], even a partial one, forms in itself a factor of disturbance potent enough to bring about, to the full extent, those harmful effects which are being witnessed in a period of depression.

How widely the two forms of investment will differ in their bearing upon the welfare of the commonwealth, may become apparent from the following comparison:

One billion dollars of savings[1], if invested in building up new capital[2], will augment the country's wealth by........	$1,000,000,000
One billion dollars of savings, if invested in the "Impairing Form," will not augment the country's wealth, but will, according to the figuring above, annihilate the income of the community to the extent of....................	$5,000,000,000

These two modes of investment, the Capitalistic and the Impairing—the one enriching the community, the other impoverishing it—may seem to counteract and exclude each other; yet they are both in action at one and the same time, especially in periods of depression, and go very well together. There may be a billion dollars invested in the Capitalistic Form and create new capital[2] to that amount, at the same time when another billion dollars is being invested in the Impairing Form, annihilating income on the part of the people to perhaps five times that amount.

* * * * * * * *

QUESTION NO. 3.—*Does the impoverishment of the community help the savers to find investment for their "Excess Savings"?*

It does. Excess Savings are invested, not in the creation of new capital, but in the acquisition of capital[2] already existing, such as the owners have to let go, owing to impoverishment; to a large extent, also, by making loans on such property, or loans to such business men as find themselves running behind.

As already stated, this process of impoverishment[9], which forms such a conspicuous feature in a depression, does not confine itself to reducing workingmen and the poorer classes to a state of privation; it will also encroach upon the wealthy, such as own property which they may realize on[10] when they can no longer defray their expenses out of their diminishing income. This process of impoverishment, therefore, will manifest itself in two distinct forms: on the one hand in the shape of privation on the part of those affected, resulting in a lowering of their standard of life; on the other hand in the shape of alienation of property.[10] These two forms of impoverishment should be kept well apart. Making a guess as to the relative proportion of these two kinds of hardship, I would say that out of a total loss of income of 5 billions due to the depression and to the lack of demand, there may be 4 billions represented by privation, and 1 billion by alienation of property.* It is the latter form of impoverishment, the loss of capital goods, which the "Basic Calculation" refers to in the early part of this chapter, when pointing out that a billion dollars of savings, if invested in a different way than in the creation of new wealth, would impoverish the non-savers of the community to the like amount of one billion. But this loss of capital goods to the amount of one billion is generally coupled with a good deal of privation, which, if expressed in money value, would represent a much larger amount. For instance, a man may lose income to the amount of $3,000 and may, in consequence, alienate property worth $1,000,[10] the loss of the remaining $2,000 being met by privation.

Strictly speaking, he would thus become poorer not by $3,000 but by $1,000. It is only the latter figure, viz., the amount represented by the alienation of property[10], which counts towards absorbing "Excess Savings." In proportion as such property is thrown upon the market, Excess Savings come to be invested, generally through the medium of some financial institution. In the purchase of such property practically all savings funds, so far as available for, but not used in, the creation of new wealth, find their outlet from the money market at times of depression. When they do, they are being spent by the receivers of the money in defraying their living expenses, and in consequence they re-enter the channels of trade and industry and are transformed into goods again. As soon as Excess Savings, say to the amount of $1,000, re-enter these channels, the harmful action caused by the

* The above proportion of 1 to 5 between "alienation of property"[10] on the one hand and "loss of income" on the other, is identical with the proportion I arrived at on page 46 as obtaining between "Excess Savings" and "loss of income." Excess Savings are equivalent in amount with the alienation[10] of property caused by the investment of such Excess Savings, so both of these factors stand in the same proportion to the third factor, "loss of income."

fact that that individual block of a thousand dollars of Excess Savings failed to be invested in the creation of new wealth, will come to an end and will not spread any further.

Excess Savings will not return into the channels of trade and industry until an equivalent alienation[10] of property on the part of non-savers has taken place, $1,000 of property against $1,000 of savings; and the impoverishment, the loss of income, forms the whip which enforces that alienation. The sooner this alienation is attained, the less need is there for the application of the whip, and the smaller is the harm brought upon the community; on the other hand, the harder people fight against the alienation of their property, and the more they meet the loss of income by privation, the fiercer will be the lash of the whip, and the greater the distress.* The more privation, the greater will be the curtailment of the demand, of consumption, and of production, and

* Let us illustrate the above by an example. Suppose a merchant has "run behind" to the amount of $1,000 in a year of depression, but withal has not reduced his business or household expenses any, making up for the deficiency by means of a loan. Such a loan, as explained before, counts the same towards absorbing Excess Savings as would an equivalent alienation of property. Here we have a case where the loss of income is **not** met by privation. Therefore the merchant's loss of $1,000 entails no diminution of the general demand and, consequently, no loss of income to others. The two factors in question, "loss of income" on the one hand and "alienation of property"[10] on the other, are coupled right in the same link of the chain and, in consequence, a multiplication of that loss of income does not take place. Now suppose the merchant acts differently, and, having anticipated a poor year, reduces his household expenses from the beginning, so as to economize $1,000 in that year. Then he meets that loss of income of $1,000 by privation to the like amount, not by alienation of property as assumed before. His economizing will reduce the general demand for commodities by $1,000; therewith production; and therewith the income of others. Then the loss of income sustained by these "others" will be at least $1,000 in addition to his own loss; but most likely those "others" will economize, too, and if so, the damage will spread from one link of the chain to the other, and may easily aggregate $5,000, **or more,** before the individuals constituting the various links of the chain have, in their entirety, sacrificed property enough to clear that amount of $1,000, or until they have become indebted that much.

The proportion between the two factors, "alienation of property" (equivalent to Excess Savings) on the one hand and "loss of income" on the other, stands as 1 to 1 in the first instance, and as 1 to 5 in the second—bearing out the statement made in the text that, the more the shrinkage of income on the part of individuals is met by privation, the more will that shrinkage of income multiply by spreading among other members of the community.

therewith of income. That whip of impoverishment will lead to both, privation as well as alienation of property; but it is only the latter which offers a bridge for Excess Savings to be invested and which thereby makes the latter return into the channels of industry and trade. Until they do return into these channels, the whip will remain in action, impoverishment will spread, and incomes will shrink.

* * * * * * * *

The conclusion arrived at in the foregoing discussion, that Excess Savings meet their investment by the mere purchase of capital goods already existing, may seem to come in conflict with an assertion made in the preceding chapter. In the reply to Explanation No. 8, page 28, I stated that the mere purchase of capital already existing, or the mere loaning out of funds on mortgage, etc., would simply shift the funds from the possession of one man to that of another, say from A to B, but would not constitute an investment of the funds *as such* the latter remaining idle, investment-seeking cash capital, now as before. While this is true where the sale is consummated as a matter of regular business, and where B intends to use the money subsequently for business purposes, i. e. for some enterprise, the situation is entirely changed if, as a new factor, the impoverishment[9] process comes into play. If B sells a bond, not for business purposes but because he needs the proceeds to defray his living expenses, then the purchase money ceases to be cash capital and *leaves the money market without going through the process of a further investment*, so that practically the real and final investment of that cash capital *is formed by the purchase of the bond.* To emphasize this point, I repeat:

Whenever capital goods are sold, and the seller uses the funds (i. e., the proceeds) for business purposes, these funds find their real and final investment when applied to such business purposes. The mere sale or purchase of property does not then constitute an investment of the funds *as such.*

Whenever capital goods are sold, and the seller expends the proceeds for living expenses, then the purchase of the property constitutes the real and final investment of the funds thus changing hands.

What is said here of cash funds in general, refers specifically to cash funds accruing from savings or surplus earnings. The latter may be invested without a creation of new wealth, simply by the purchase of capital[2] already existing, provided a concurrent impoverishment[9] of the owners of that capital takes place. Otherwise the transaction does not constitute an investment.

Let us illustrate this point still further by an example. Suppose a wage earner, H, loses his position and therewith his income. He owns a house, worth say $5,000. From his friend A, a saver, he borrows some money which he uses for his living expenses; and when through with it he borrows again, paying interest accordingly. After running his debt up to $1,000, he gives A a mortgage on the house; which mortgage is subsequently increased to $2,000 and to $3,000, in proportion as his indebtedness grows. H may find employment again after that. But the debt remains, and constitutes a profitable, interest-bearing investment for A's savings. Here we have a plain case showing how savings can be employed without the creation of new capital goods; also, how the impoverishment of the non-savers actually ***forms the basis of the investment***, opening up, as it were, a new field for investments, just at a time when depression prevails and when poverty is spreading, and when the ***regular*** field of investment narrows down. The example also explains the mysterious disappearance of the savings funds from the money market at times of depression: Had the mortgage been given for ***business*** purposes, there would be a cash capital of $3,000 in H's hands to show for it; or, eventually, there would be a new construction of some kind to show for the ***cash capital***, in case H invested it. In the case covered by our example, however, there will be no available cash capital of $3,000 when H issues the mortgage, most of the money having already been spent by him, and no new property having been created with the aid of it. The funds gradually disappeared from the money market without leading to any visible result—just as we see it in real life.

It is in the acquisition of property which the owners cannot hold, that Excess Savings find their final investment; either directly, by outright purchase, or indirectly, by acquiring a title to or a lien on such property, say in the shape of a mortgage or of a common loan. The characteristic feature of the investment of Excess Savings is the *Change of Possession* of property (capital goods) already existing, in conjunction with the involuntary impoverishment of the previous owner. This kind of investment is going on, to a small extent, even at prosperous times; but it grows in extent as business relaxes, and at times of serious depression will actually be the predominating form of investment.

* * * * * * * *

Let us recapitulate the three queries raised in the early part of this chapter in connection with the "Basic Calculation" and in connection with the process of impoverishment[9] which that calculation reveals. Our first query was, *whether such improverishment really exists, at times of depression.* No economist will seriously attempt to deny that it does. Second query: *How is that impoverishment brought about?* By lack of employment and lack of earnings. At times of depression but little in the line of new constructions is being built up, in consequence of which fact the Constructive Working

Forces,[7] which I designated as class C, are largely put to idleness and are thus deprived of their earnings. This enforced idleness will spread further, reacting on the "Commodity Working Forces" D, E, F, etc., engaged in production and trade, and will reduce their income also, thus bringing about a multiplication of the annihilation of income, aggregating perhaps five times the original loss sustained by the forces C. This annihilation of income will, on the one hand, lead to more or less privation on the part of the classes C, D, E, F, etc.; on the other hand to alienation of property[10] on the part of the wealthy members of these classes. Third query: ***Does this annihilation of income, and the consequent impoverishment of a large part of the community, help the savers to find investment for their surplus earnings, such as are not absorbed in the creation of new wealth?*** It does. This class of surplus earnings finds its investment in the purchase of property or capital goods which the owners are compelled to alienate[10] as a sequence of that impoverishment. Without the impoverishment there would be no such forced alienation of property, and without the latter there would not be the opportunities for investing "Excess Savings."

* * * * * * * *

Economists will not dispute that now and then the impoverishment of the one individual will enable the other to invest his savings by merely purchasing property already existing. They may also admit that such cases occur more frequently in seasons of depression, where incomes shrink and where the impoverishment process becomes more pronounced. But to admit that this impoverishment process should go far enough to absorb practically all surplus income that is not absorbed in the creation of new wealth; and that, moreover, the impoverishment should be a matter of inherent necessity in order to provide investment for that class of surplus income—to admit that, would be almost impossible for our economists, unless they thoroughly remodel the accepted theories on the subject of saving. Still, it is hard to avoid those conclusions, which coincide with the conclusion arrived at in the "Basic Calculation" given on page 40, viz.: if the savers become richer and the total wealth of the community does not increase to an equal extent, the non-savers must become poorer, and either must give up property or become indebted, to the full amount of the "Excess Savings."

In the foregoing pages it has been shown how a deficiency of the demand is created in the interval between the act of saving and the act of investment, provided the latter takes place in the Impairing Form[8]—a deficiency which is never compensated for by the act of investment. The conclusions arrived at may seem to run counter to a well-established axiom of modern economics, That the shortage of the demand originally caused by the act of saving is always compensated for by the act of investment, provided the savings funds finally come to be expended for goods or services in the course of such investment. Whether this axiom can stand scrutiny or not, will be discussed in a subsequent chapter. For the present let us bear in mind that much depends upon the manner in which the savings funds come into the possession of the individuals who expend them for commodities and thus turn them into goods again—whether in the shape of income, in payment for services rendered, or whether over the bridge of their own impoverishment, in the shape of loans, or as the proceeds of property which they were compelled to alienate or realize on.

CHAPTER IV.

VARIOUS DEPRESSION THEORIES.

IN the preceding chapters the cause of depressions has been connected with a relaxation in the process of building up new capital.[2] That such a relaxation actually sets in concurrently with the beginning of a depression is generally admitted by economists; and it is also understood that as a consequence the working forces ordinarily engaged in said process are largely reduced to idleness—also that this forced idleness reacts upon those engaged in the broad lines of production and upon business in general, thus aggravating the ill effects originally caused by the subsidence of new undertakings. But while this slackening of new constructions is well known to be the immediate cause of depressions, it is also well understood not to be the primary cause, being itself a sequence of causes still more remote. The nature of the real, the primary cause, has been a subject of much discussion among economists, many theories being extant to explain the origin of that lull in new constructions. Let us review some of these theories.

DEPRESSION THEORY NO. 1.

(LACK OF FUNDS.)

The fact that a dearth of cash capital, when becoming acute, is likely to engender a crisis, and will always form a conspicuous feature of the crisis proper after it once sets in, has led many economists to believe that the depression following a crisis must likewise be attributed to that cause, i. e., to the lack of funds. This view has been discussed at some length in Chapter I, where I have pointed out that though a dearth of cash capital will often engender a crisis and serve to usher in the subsequent depression, it can not be the cause of the continuance of the latter, inasmuch as we generally do not find a scarcity of cash capital after the depression has properly developed and passed the primary stage. The obvious fact that some other and more powerful element must intervene to give continuity to the depression, since the primary factor—the dearth of cash capital—is no longer active, this fact should conclusively disprove the "lack-of-funds" theory, provided we are looking for the inherent cause of the *depression*, and not merely for the origin of the *crisis*. On the other hand, such an array of brilliant arguments has been brought forward in support of the lack-of-funds theory, arguments which may seem largely to controvert my own conclusions, that I deem it best to take up some of them and expose their fallacy.

Almost all of these arguments lose sight of an important point, namely, that productive capital[2] can not forever go on increasing. The most natural explanation of the cause of depressions, such as would readily occur to a business man, would probably be this: "Productive capital can not keep on growing forever; it can expand only in proportion as the demand for the products of capital expands, and this demand is almost always lagging behind. The growth of productive capital, therefore, is checked because the demand cannot follow."

This explanation, however, has not found much favor among economists, their views trending rather in the opposite direction. Most of them prefer to attribute the check in the formation of productive capital, not to the superabundance of capital[2] already in existence, but to the shortage of liquid capital such as is necessary to build up still more of it. Their chief arguments may be summed up in the following four points:

ARGUMENT NO. 1.—The alleged superabundance of productive capital has existed in the past pretty much the same as it does today. As this superabundance heretofore did not hinder the growth of productive capital, there is no reason why it should do so at present, or in the future. Going by the experience of the past we must conclude that in spite of that superabundance of productive capital there is always room for more.

ARGUMENT NO. 2.—The expansion of productive capital is to a certain extent self-sustaining. The more capital there is, the greater the general demand; and in turn, the more the demand grows, the greater the need of productive capital.

ARGUMENT NO. 3.—Whenever the investment process relaxes, the cause thereof must be due to either one of two alternatives, either to a lack of opportunities for profitable investment, or to a lack of savings funds to be invested. Which of these two causes is the predominating one? If it were the former, i. e., if the opportunities for investment were wanting, the savings funds would accumulate in the money market in the shape of huge idle cash funds, which as we know is not the case. The cause of the relaxation, therefore, must be due to the other alternative, i. e., to the lack of savings funds available for investment—a conclusion fully corroborated by the fact that savings almost always can find investment of a reasonably profitable character.

ARGUMENT NO. 4.—A period of very active business and of rapid increase of productive capital uses up the savings funds faster than they accrue and will even draw heavily upon the resources of all credit institutions, so much so that towards the end of such a period we find a considerable dearth of liquid capital. A period of relaxation, therefore, is bound to follow in order to replenish the stock of liquid capital necessary for a subsequent period of expansion and of new enterprises.

Let us examine the four arguments above given, to

see if they can stand scrutiny; and let us take them up in reversed rotation, the last point first.

REPLY TO ARGUMENT NO. 4.—The scarcity of cash funds, often noticed towards the end of a "boom" period, is due largely to the fact that during that period prices and wages undergo a gradual rise, in consequence of which more money is needed for industry and trade. If towards the end of a "boom" period, a general rise of, say, 15 per cent. has been effected, the transaction of the country's business may call for 10 to 15 per cent. more of the circulating medium. To procure the additional cash thus needed, business men look to the money market, and in consequence a larger part of the savings which constantly flow in and which otherwise would be available for new enterprises, is absorbed for purposes of regular business. Even without this rise in prices or wages there is more of the circulating medium required in a time of active business than in a dull time. These two factors, in addition to the steady absorption of cash funds for the sake of launching new enterprises, account for the scarcity of liquid capital so often noticed previous to the setting in of a crisis.*

As to the theory that a period of relaxation and of forced economy is necessary to replenish the stock of liquid capital which would be required for another "boom" period, I refer to the discussions following Explanations Nos. 1, 2, 3, 4 and 5 in Chapter II. In those Explanations I have considered every imaginable form in which this replenishing process possibly may assume practical shape, and have shown that all of those Explanations lose sight of the enormous amounts, running into billions, which we have to deal with when trying to explain what becomes of the surplus earnings, available

* A further factor which, at times, contributes towards creating a scarcity of cash funds, will be discussed on page 161.

for investment, which accrue in the course of several years of depression. The view most current is, that such funds lie over in the shape of "loanable funds." Let us fully understand the meaning of this word "loanable"; it does not mean funds "loaned out" (for that would imply funds which *have found* employment), but funds *ready to be employed*, and in the meantime lying idle. The adherents of this view altogether fail to consider that such loanable funds would, first of all, show up in the commercial banks; that, inasmuch as they remain unemployed, they would rapidly accumulate there to a stupendous amount; that each year of sharp depression, such as prevailed in the United States from 1893 to 1897, would add hardly less than one billion dollars to the idle funds of the country, making an aggregate of four billions for the four years—while as a matter of fact the banks showed only an insignificant increase of their loanable funds at the end of that period, in 1897, as compared with 1892. All of these facts, which have been fully discussed in Chapter II, disprove the above stated view as to the usefulness of a period of depression in increasing the country's liquid capital or replenishing the funds depleted in the preceding "boom" period.

REPLY TO ARGUMENT NO. 3.—The latter has so far been considered unanswerable. It seems plausible to infer that if savings funds available for capitalistic investment, that is, for the creation of new wealth, did not find their employment to that end, they would accumulate in the money market; and inasmuch as no such accumulation takes place, it has been assumed that sooner or later they really do find investment in the capital-producing form. It must be conceded that if this latter form were the only one in existence for investing such funds, this argument would be conclusive. But it is not the only form. In Chapter III it has been shown that the savings funds are not confined to investment in the Capitalistic Form, but often find it in the Impairing Form—a fact which completely upsets Argument 3.

REPLY TO ARGUMENT NO. 2.—There is some truth in the assertion that the growth of productive capital is in a certain way self-sustaining, inasmuch as this growth is followed by an enlarged demand for commodities. But that demand will not grow *in the same proportion*. If it did, there would not be that universal excess of productive capital above the demand for it. This excess exists in spite of the fact that there are times when it seems to disappear and when the demand for commodities grows large enough to keep the productive capital fairly well employed. Such keen demand is not normal, but is fostered by special circumstances. It occurs, strange to say, just at seasons when a rapid increase of productive capital takes place; and, what is still more strange, it is caused by the very act of building up such productive capital. By that act, so long as it lasts, the general demand is temporarily stimulated. Capitalists who are building new railroads, factories, houses, machinery, &c., *become consumers for the time being*, inasmuch as they engage working forces to a large extent and thus increase the general demand; when through building, however, and when about to set their works agoing, they become producers where they were consumers and are thus beginning to increase the supply and to decrease the demand. A multitude of such cases will result in a growing disparity between demand and supply and will therewith re-establish that relative superabundance of productive capital which forms the normal state of affairs.

Boom periods, where the demand almost equals the supply, are always accompanied by a rapid increase of productive capital, and are, in fact *caused* by this **rapid** increase. Were this increase self-sustaining, as assumed in Argument No. 2; in other words, were the growth of productive capital followed by a corresponding growth of the demand, then there would be no reason why the demand, after a while, should lag behind. The fact that it does lag shows conclusively its inability to keep pace with the growing powers of production.

REPLY TO ARGUMENT NO. 1.—There are many economists who reject the idea that the alleged superabundance of productive capital should form a barrier against the still further growth of such capital. They hold that all arguments in that direction are met by the simple fact that capital[2], in spite of that barrier, is constantly increasing *and that there is room for the increase*—a point which indeed sounds plausible and unanswerable. In reality, however, this point is no more conclusive than would be the assertion that our civil laws form no barrier against crime, on the plea that these laws are constantly being trespassed against. The barrier is not an absolute one in either case; still it exists, and is eminently effective. The superabundance of capital[2] forms no *absolute* barrier against its increase, but it keeps that increase within narrow limits, such as are drawn *by the extent of the demand for the products of capital.* If more capital exists in any special line than necessary to meet the demand, and if the excess should surpass a certain proportion, say 15 or 20 per cent., that excess will certainly put a stop to the further increase of capital in that line, except in sporadic cases where an enterprising capitalist has, or thinks he has, special advantages for competing.

Were that barrier not in existence, and were the growth of productive capital merely dependent upon the supply of savings funds applicable to that purpose, capital would, long before this, have grown to an extent beyond all conception. An idea of the rapidity with which capital would expand under such circumstances may be gained from the following examples:

EXAMPLE NO. 1.—As is well known, a penny loaned out at the time of Christ at a moderate rate of compound interest, and accumulating undisturbed, would now have grown to an amount impossible to pay. If we consider that at present there are funds amounting to many billions of dollars loaned out or invested, and growing on the compound interest principle, the question arises, can these funds keep on growing at that ratio for any great length of time? If we consider furthermore that the elements of insecurity which in past ages hampered the continued accumulation and conservation of capital are being more and more eliminated, and if we consider that on this account the accumulation process goes on all the more rapidly—is it not evident that the accumulation must reach the limit of the possible much sooner than in the case of the penny—and must indeed reach it within a comparatively short time?

EXAMPLE NO. 2.—In prosperous years the people of the United States save up and turn into capital[2] about one-seventh of their income. For the ten years from 1880 to 1890 the income has been estimated at an average of 14 billions per annum, and if we figure the savings at one-seventh of this amount—that is, 2 billions annually for ten years—we arrive at an aggregate of 20 billions. This amount approximates the actual gain in wealth which, according to Census reports, took place in that period, viz., from 43 billions in 1880 to 65 billions in 1890. For the ten years from 1890 to 1900, which included only six years of prosperity, the increase has been variously estimated at from 23 to 29 billions, which again would represent a saving power of about one-seventh of the people's aggregate income, figuring the latter at 20 billions, on the average. Could such a rate of accumulation, growing larger from year to year, be kept up for a long time, say, for centuries in succession?

EXAMPLE NO. 3.—If the people of the United States can, under favorable circumstances, accumulate one-seventh of their income, though they are not regarded as possessing much of a propensity for saving, how much larger ought to be the savings and the accumulated wealth of such thrifty peoples as the Dutch and the French! If we figure only a ratio of 10 per cent. of their income which, under favorable circumstances, they could put by, and carry the calculation back for three or four centuries, starting with any sum half way within the limits of the probable as representing the people's annual income at that time, the total accumulated wealth should be many times greater than it really is—especially so if we consider that the annual increase in wealth will increase the people's income, and, in turn, the increased income will augment the people's saving power, and therewith the annual accumulation. In view of this reciprocal action, all tending toward an enlargement of the country's wealth, we would be fully justified in figuring the growth of the latter on the compound interest principle, and if so, we would find a stupendous discrepancy between the wealth there is and the wealth there ought to be.

These three examples should be sufficient to demonstrate the enormous cumulative power of the saving process—provided this cumulative principle had free scope. It is well understood, however, that it has not. But why not? In the case of the penny referred to in Example 1, we all know the reason—social and political disturbances of the most radical character, which made it impossible for any aggregation of capital to survive. In the case of France and Holland it may also be held that the discrepancy above mentioned can be fully accounted for by wars and other disturbing influences. But the damage from wars—devastation of property, and war expenses, sustained by Holland and France in the course of several centuries—would represent only an insignificant proportion of that discrepancy; and a still smaller proportion would be represented by disturbing factors other than war Excepting these temporary adversities, the *extraneous* conditions should have been favorable and should have allowed a rapid accumulation of wealth, in proportion to the people's saving power. If nevertheless that rapid accumulation did not materialize there must have been a hidden cause at work to prevent it—a cause which despite the favorable *extraneous* conditions created unfavorable *inherent* conditions sufficient to check the cumulative power and therewith the growth of wealth and of productive capital. Just so with the United States. Its rapid rate of increase in wealth can not continue forever. It will be restrained by the same factor which has limited the accumulation process in the older countries.

We need not look far to find this factor—it consists of the fact that ordinarily the extent of the productive capital already in existence exceeds the demand therefor, thus curtailing the incentive for building up still more of it. This almost continuous superabundance of capital, which has been a characteristic feature of past ages as well as of recent times, reduces the opportunities for profitable investment, and thereby forms a most effective barrier against the unlimited creation of new productive capital.

Economists are not generally inclined to consider this natural barrier in the proper light, and prefer to believe that such a barrier either must be an absolute one, or that it does not exist at all. Many of them seem to hold that so long as there is a house left to be built, or any sort of enterprise still to be carried out, so long can there be no lack of opportunities for profitable investment of billions of savings funds and, therefore, no barrier. That the latter is only relative and not absolute seems to have escaped their attention. They are unaware of the fact that whenever, on account of this barrier, the opportunities for profitable investment in new constructions become scarce, only a part of the savings funds will find investment in that form—the balance simply being diverted to the Impairing Form, as explained in Chapter III.

* * * * * * * *

Of the four arguments considered above, which form the chief support of what we properly may call the "Lack-of-Funds" theory, not one can stand scrutiny. The "boundless opportunities" for the expansion of productive capital do not exist. On the contrary, wherever opportunities turn up for safe and half-way profitable investment, there is, ordinarily, no lack of savings funds to make use of them. And though there may be periods where this truth does not seem to hold good, and where the great demand for new constructions creates a demand for cash funds far in excess of the possible supply—as has recently been the case in the United States and in Germany—it is well understood that such exceptional periods will not last and that sooner or later the ordinary state of affairs, the excess of productive capital over and above the demand for it, will reassert itself. As soon as it does, there is no longer a scarcity of funds such as are available for new enterprises.

While the lack-of-funds theory will undoubtedly account for the origin of most of our *crises*, as set forth in Chapter I, it will not account for the period of continued depression which so often follows the crisis.

DEPRESSION THEORY NO. 2.

(EXCESSIVE PROFITS.)

This theory makes a sharp distinction between the wealthy classes and the working classes, ascribing to the latter the greater consumptive power and to the former the greater accumulating power. Thus, for illustration, out of an income of $20,000 going into the hands *of the working classes,* more than $19,000 are likely to be expended for consumptibles and less than $1,000 to be accumulated; while out of the same income, if going into the hands of the wealthy, only $10,000 may be spent and as much as $10,000 accumulated. Evidently, therefore, the larger the share which out of the people's total income goes to the working classes, the greater the demand for consumptibles; and again, the larger the share which goes to the wealthy, the greater the accumulation; and inasmuch as the accumulations generally are turned into productive capital (i. e., into capital which produces commodities), we also might say, *the greater the production of commodities*. A plentiful income on the part of the working classes and of the masses, therefore, favors the demand, while a plentiful income on the part of the wealthy favors the supply. The theory ascribes the generally existing disparity between demand and supply to the fact that the share of income received by the working classes is too small, that of the wealthy too large.

This faulty division, as the theory has it, occasions no disturbance in times of general prosperity, since at such times the deficiency of the demand on the part of the working classes (due to the deficiency of their income) is compensated for by the increased demand emanating from the wealthy, the latter investing their surplus earnings in the creation of new wealth and productive capital, and therewith bringing an increased demand for working forces into the market. At such times, therefore, the working forces are well employed. After a number of years, however, the rapid creation of new productive capital will slacken, as the demand can not follow, and then the consequences of the above-mentioned faulty division manifest themselves in the shape of a growing preponderance of the supply, culminating in a depression.

* * * * * * * *

There is much truth in the foregoing theory, and in itself it is not antagonistic to the true cause of depressions, such as will be developed in the next chapter; but it does not go far enough, and falls short of discerning the primary cause. We may conceive a state of affairs where that faulty division of income is carried to extremes and where the working classes practically receive no income at all, being kept like slaves, and still business would prosper provided the wealthy would expend the enormous accessions to their income either for luxuries, or in the steady expansion of new capital[2] and wealth. Evidently, therefore, that faulty division of income is not in itself sufficient to cause a depression, but some other more potent factor must come into play to lead to that result.

The theory acknowledges the fact that the faulty division will do no harm so long as the funds accruing from the savings and surplus earnings of the wealthy are invested in the creation of new productive capital, and thus give employment to the working forces engaged in that line. But the theory overlooks the natural question. If the funds, though not applied towards new constructions, are invested in some *other* way, why do they not give employment to some other class of working forces? If in either case the savings funds meet real investment, such as will cause them finally to be dissolved and to be paid over to working men and business men in the purchase of commodities, why should there be prosperous conditions and full employment for the working forces in the one case and unemployment in the other? If it is the different mode of investment which entails the unemployment and the stagnation in trade, the matter should be explained, for then the cause of the trouble evidently lies right here, not in the faulty division of income.

As a matter of fact the "Excessive-Profits" theory connects the cause of depressions with the saving process, holding that the over-abundant profits and income of the wealthy stimulate that process to an undue extent and therewith the excessive construction of new productive capital—and in this respect there is much truth in the theory. But it does not show us in what manner the deleterious influence of the saving process takes place, and therefore falls short of discerning the direct and immediate cause of depressions. It loses sight of two important questions; first: If, at times of depression, the savings funds do not find investment, where are they, since they do not show up in the money market; and again: If they do find investment, why do they not give employment to working forces, and why should the latter be so largely condemned to idleness?

* * * * * * * *

There is another version of Theory No. 2; as it were, a modification of same, which limits itself substantially to the point that the production of such consumptibles as are used by the working classes absorbs and employs more working forces than are required in the production of such commodities as are consumed by the wealthy; in other words, that $1,000 expended for the common necessaries of life would bring more working forces into action than $1,000 expended for luxuries; and that for this reason the faulty division of income above referred to works injuriously. If we thus limit the scope of the theory, it is still less apparent why the said factor should show its ill effects only at times of depression, or why it should lead to a depression at one time and not at another. Nor is the very starting point of this version of the theory correct. True, the manufacture of $1,000 worth of luxuries calls for a smaller number of workers than would the production of $1,000 worth of necessaries; but we have to bear in mind that the individuals producing the luxuries will, on their part, when expending their income, create a demand for *common* necessaries. And when adding the latter class of demand to the other it is not apparent why there should be any deficiency in the aggregate.

DEPRESSION THEORY NO. 3.

(DISPROPORTIONS.)

The fundamental part of this theory hinges on disproportions existing between economic factors; too much of the one, too little of the other. There may be a disproportion (1) between the various lines of production; (2) between the aggregates of city population and country population; (3) between the volume of capital flowing into some lines of business and that flowing into other lines; (4) between the income of the wealthy and that of the working classes; (5) between the volume of productive capital and the demand for its products—and in fact between many other economic factors such as ought to maintain due proportions to one another.

In sum and substance Theory No. 3 ascribes economic disturbances to a lack of system in productive activity—to the absence of a governing power controlling production and distribution which would cause the various economic factors to work harmoniously with each other.

* * * * * * * *

When examining the various forms of disproportion

enumerated above, we first ought to eliminate those given under Nos. 4 and 5—the one having been already treated of under "Theory No. 2," page 66, and the other being so closely related to the main theme of this treatise as not to require especial consideration in this place. As a matter of fact, Theory No. 3 is generally understood to confine itself chiefly to such factors as relate to the broad fields of production. Limiting our discussion accordingly, and weighing the pros and cons as to whether depressions and disturbances can really be traced to disproportions of this nature, the following objections would present themselves:

OBJECTION NO. 1.—That there is, in many lines of business, an excess of the *means* of production cannot be doubted; but is there an excess of *actual production?* Is not the so-called over-production becoming more and more a matter of the past, and does not production under modern conditions adjust itself very closely to the demand? Take, for instance, iron and steel, the output of which a few years ago attained enormous proportions in the United States—did not the production promptly decline with the diminution of the demand in 1903 and 1904? Was there, at any time, a real overproduction in this line, or in any other line of manufacture, that did not speedily correct itself?* If we find a close adjustment of the supply to the demand to obtain everywhere,

* A seeming exception to this rule may be found in the production of copper in the United States, enormous over-supplies having come to light in 1903 and again in 1907. In both instances, however, the overproduction was intentional, forming part of a scheme for manipulating the stock market. While the overproduction went on, an artificial scarcity of the metal was created by means of hiding a part of the output out of sight, the public being made to believe that all of the enormous production was quickly selling at excessive prices. On the strength of this belief the shares of the copper mining companies advanced to high figures and were then unloaded by the "insiders" on this inflated basis. When the truth became known, and the over-supplies came to light, an enormous drop of prices ensued, not only in the metal but more so in the shares, which enabled the insiders to buy their shares back at half the price they had sold them at. Such manipulative overproduction does not disprove the rule stated in the text above.

we evidently have no right to assert that there is too much production going on in the one line of business and too little in the other. Or take as another kind of disproportion the flocking of the country people into the cities—is not the main reason for this migration to be found in the fact that city work pays better than farm work? And if so, does not this migration rather tend to *correct* a disproportion than to create one? Finally, referring to the third kind of disproportions mentioned above, is there much truth in the oft-repeated assertion that too much cash capital is flowing into some lines of business, and too little into others? Do not investors naturally select such lines of business as are least overrun, and which therefore give best promise of adequate returns? True, such a promise may subsequently fail of fulfillment, owing to a falling off of the demand. For example, prior to 1903 much cash capital went into the construction of iron and steel plants in the United States, and when later on the demand for the product of these plants fell off, much was heard about the expansion having been out of proportion to the real requirements. But did such disproportion exist at the time the investments were made?

The gist of Theory No. 3 is represented by the assumption that a partial overproductive engenders a general overproduction. But if the former does not exist, how can the general overproduction be ascribed to it?

OBJECTION NO. 2.—If we were to believe that the maintenance of proper proportions between the various lines of production insures prosperous times and a disproportion leads to the opposite result, we might ask the question, Did the business men of the United States exercise good judgment in this direction all through the thirteen years of prosperity from 1880 to 1893, while in the subsequent four years of depression they failed to do likewise? The supposition which this question implies is simply preposterous, and Theory No. 3 certainly cannot stand where it leads to such conclusions. As a matter of fact, the business men acted just as intelligently at the one period as the other, and at either time did their best to adjust their production to the requirements of the market.

True, there is one line of production that is in a great measure beyond control by human foresight, and where the annual output therefore may vary considerably; that is, agriculture. The products of agriculture represent such a large share of the total production that their scarcity or abundance should certainly affect the aggregate in the manner assumed in Theory No. 3, were that theory correct. As a matter of fact, however, we find a poor crop to occur now and then in a period of prosperity, and a good crop while times are bad, but as a rule the general drift of business is not reversed by such occurrences. If overproduction in such an important line as agriculture fails to turn the tide, how can we expect such a result from *other* lines, which are on the one hand less important and on the other far more within human control?

OBJECTION NO. 3.—Obviously the principle of disproportion, as enunciated in Theory No. 3, could be held responsible for depressions only if it could be proved to lead to a diminution of the general demand.

Theory No. 3 attempts such a proof on the following line of reasoning: In one or some lines of business there occurs an overproduction, or at least excessive competition. In consequence, prices in those lines will fall; therewith the income of the respective producers; and therewith their purchasing power. Owing to this lessening of the purchasing power on the part of these individuals the producers in all other lines of business cannot sell them so much as before; therefore these other lines will also suffer, and the partial overproduction becomes a general one.

Let us see how far this line of reasoning can stand scrutiny. To this end let us select some special trade, say, the shoe business, and let us assume, for the sake of argument, that this industry embraces 10 per cent. of all the working forces[6] of the community. Let us designate the people so engaged as Group D; the remaining 90 per cent., embracing all other lines of business, as Group S. Suppose the first-named group be compelled, by sharp competition, to reduce the selling price of shoes by 20 per cent.; will the members of the other group (S) really suffer thereby and find their purchasing power lessened?

To investigate this question, let us further assume the purchasing power of the whole community to be $1,000 per annum, of which $900 comes from Group S and $100 from Group D. Now, suppose that the break in prices above referred to, sets in, and that Group D will subsequently realize only $80 for their goods (shoes) instead of $100 as before; which means that the purchasing power of Group D is lessened by $20. Evidently the members of Group S will now spend less money for shoes. If their expenditures on this account had formerly been $90 per annum, they can now buy the same goods for $72, and have $18 over, *which amount becomes available for buying other kinds of commodities*, additional to those theretofore purchased by that group. This increased purchasing power on the part of Group S will give employment to a third group, T, to the amount of $18, and the latter group will at once become a purchaser to that extent and will fully make up for the reduced purchasing power of Group D. Even the seeming discrepancy between the surplus of $18 coming to Group S as against the loss of $20 sustained by Group D, disappears when considering that the members of the latter group, who so far have been spending $10 per annum to buy what they themselves needed in the line of shoes, can now buy what they need for $8, so that their real loss of purchasing power comes to only $18, not $20.

Now let us figure the totals. Owing to excessive competition among those employed in the shoe business, their purchasing power becomes reduced from $100 to $82; that of all other classes rises from $900 to $918; making an aggregate of $1000. Before the sharp competition set in, the aggregate purchasing power amounted also to $1000. Where, then, does the falling off of the demand come in?

Thus when going into details and resorting to figures, we find no substantial basis for the assertion that the cheapening of some lines of goods, caused by a partial overproduction or by excessive competition, in any line of industry, should lessen the purchasing power of the community as a whole, or reduce the aggregate of the demand. Just the reverse takes place—the cheapening of any line of goods will *benefit* the community ond increase its purchasing power—perhaps not in terms of money, but certainly in the volume of goods which the money will command. * * * * * * * *

When speaking of overproduction, economists often do not mean excessive production of the commodities as such (which, as stated before, is more and more becoming a matter of the past) but an excess of the *means* for production. By overproduction in any special line they mostly mean an excess of *productive capital* in that line. And it is the alleged disproportion in building up productive capital, too much in the one branch of industry and too little in the other, to which they principally ascribe the derangement of business and the resultant depression.

But a depression cannot take place without a falling off of the demand: and why the demand should suffer owing to the said disproportion, that has never been proved. Any attempt to establish such a proof would at once come to naught when trying to substantiate it by means of figures.

Suppose there be an excess of cash funds invested in the creation of bicycle plants and too little in shoe factories; true, this disproportion will result in a lessened demand for working forces so far as the building of shoe factories is concerned, but will not this be fully compensated for by the increased demand arising from the building up of the bicycle plants? And if the said disproportion will not reduce the demand while *building* the factories, have we more reason to believe that it will do so later on, when *operating* them? It might be held that while part of the bicycle plants would stand idle for lack of work, there would not be shoe factories enough to meet the demand for shoes, and to give employment to the hands required to supply this demand. But if such were the case, we should expect to see on the one hand a sharp rise in the price of shoes and on the other hand a lack of cash funds available for building up new factories in this line—while as a matter of fact we find neither the one nor the other, in *any* line of business, except under unusual circumstances. Where are those lines of industry which offer opportunities for safe and paying investment at times of depression, and for which the funds to make use of such opportunities cannot be obtained?

Here we encounter the vulnerable point of the theory that too much cash capital goes into the one line of business and too little in the other. Were this assumption true, the neglected line should be noted for high prices and scarcity of supply, as the only possible result of that disproportion. The adherents of said theory, however, argue the other way, and contend that the lack of investment funds going into the neglected line, and the consequent restriction of the means of production, would result, not in high prices and scarcity of the supply but in overproduction and low prices—a paradoxical conclusion, to say the least.

Out of the great number of theories which economists have brought forth to explain the cause of depressions, I have, in the foregoing pages, been discussing the three which count the greatest number of adherents. All these theories ascribe the depression to the relaxation of new constructions, differing, however, as to the causes of this relaxation; the one theory assigning it to a lack of the funds necessary to keep up the rapid expansion of productive capital, such as took place in the preceding "boom" period; the other assigning the relaxation to the excessive income of the wealthy classes, which is thought to lead to an excessive construction of new productive capital and to an undue stimulation of the supply, so much so that in course of time the demand can no longer keep pace with the supply; the third theory assigning the relaxation to a disproportion between the economic factors that should maintain an equilibrium in order to avoid overproduction. But while each one of these theories regards the lull in new constructions as being an indispensable prerequisite for the setting in of the depression, this lull, as will be shown later on, is neither the direct and immediate cause of it, nor indeed an indispensable prerequisite. I repeat that if we recognize the true cause of depressions and find the means of removing it, the process of new constructions might practically come to a standstill, and yet business would prosper.

CHAPTER V.

THE "NEGLECTED POINT" AS THE TRUE CAUSE OF DEPRESSIONS.

IN Chapter 3 it has been shown that savings, such as are available for investment, will, in times of depression, find investment in the Capitalistic (capital-producing) Form only to a limited extent, the balance finding it in the Impairing Form. It has also been shown that, if they are so invested, a diminution of the demand, with all its ill effects, is the inevitable result.

Now I wish to emphasize that when speaking of the "Impairing Form of Investment" this term should not be understood as attributing these ill effects to the investment as such, the act of investing being invariably beneficent, from an economic standpoint, inasmuch as it restores the savings funds to the channels of industry and trade, thereby preventing the hoarding of funds and the strain resulting therefrom which would otherwise be entailed by the saving process.

Seemingly there is a contradiction in the two foregoing paragraphs, one of them stating that the investment, if made in the Impairing Form, means a diminution of the demand; the other, that the investment as such will not lead to a diminution of the demand. Some light may be thrown on this seeming contradiction, however, if we bear in mind that the act of investing is a sequence of the act of saving, these two acts being often considered as mere phases of the accumulation process. Can the disturbing element, if not due to the investment process, be charged to the saving process?

Is it possible that the saving activity as such can

exercise any injurious influence in the direction of curtailing the demand—that is, the demand for working forces?

All economists agree that it can. In its primary stage the saving process is always accompanied by an injurious tendency, inasmuch as the saver is constantly trying to buy less from the community in the line of goods or services than he sells to it, and thus is disturbing the equilibrium of supply and demand. This equilibrium is restored only by the investment. It is understood that by means of the investment the demand for goods or services —i. e., for working forces[6]—will reappear in the market. Thus, if somebody saves $1,000 he will first create what we might call a "minus of demand" to the extent of $1,000. But whenever he invests his savings, say, in building a house, the money is spent for labor, for production of the necessary material, supervision, etc.; so he transforms the $1,000 into wages and profits, i. e., into income for others, and in doing so he employs working forces and creates a demand for them fully sufficient to couterbalance the minus of demand referred to above.

But while this restoration of the equilibrium between supply and demand will undoubtedly take place under the Capitalistic Form of investment, that is, where new constructions of some kind are being created, will it also take place under the Impairing Form, where, as we have seen in Chapter 3, the act of investment will not call for working forces? Will the minus of demand, and the consequent unemployment, as originally caused by the act of saving, be wiped out by the act of investment, where the latter brings no demand for working forces with it? Certainly not. Under such circumstances the injurious tendency connected with the primary stage of the saving process is no longer counterbalanced, *and if not counterbalanced it will go into effect.* This being the case, it must be the saving activity, not the investment, to which are due the harmful results that follow. The mode of investment merely determines whether those harmful tendencies inherent in the saving process become operative or not. They certainly will become operative whenever they are no longer counteracted by the investment, i. e., whenever the latter assumes the Impairing Form.

To recall to our mind the modus operandi of that peculiar form of investment, let us repeat its salient points, as developed in Chapter 3.

Whenever the Impairing Form of Investment prevails, as is the case in times of depression, the savers do not apply their funds in such a way as to turn them into income for those whom the funds go to. They do not buy personal services with the money, nor goods for consumption, because that would be *spending* the money, whereas they mean to *save* it; nor do they (or others for them) invest it in building up new productive capital, because new enterprises rarely pay in times of depression. They need not do either, and still they can invest their funds; the opportunities for doing so turning up in a rather roundabout way. Inasmuch as they abstain from going into new constructions, the group of working forces[6] ordinarily employed in such constructions is reduced to idleness. The income of these working forces diminishes accordingly. The loss of income means a lessening of their purchasing power; this, a slackening of the demand for commodities; this again, a curtailment of the *production* of such commodities and a lack of employment for the producers and distributors of same. Thus the enforced idleness of the first-mentioned group of working forces, the "Constructive Forces," will react upon another group, in the line of the "Commodity Working Forces[7]," reducing them to idleness also (at least to some extent), and this process of action and reaction will spread from the second group to the third, from there to the fourth, to the fifth, and so on, bringing with it in every instance a diminution of the demand and a corresponding annihilation of income, and thus causing a considerable multiplication of the ill effects and of the unemployment sustained by the first group. The loss of income of, say, $1,000 on the part of the first group may, by reason of this "Multiplying Principle", be augmented to a total loss of income of perhaps $3,000, or $4,000 or $5,000 (varying according to circumstances), distributed among many groups of individuals.

These groups are composed not only of working men but also include business men, many of whom find their trade and their income more or less curtailed, and in consequence are "running behind" where they used to make a profit. To meet their expenses, they find themselves compelled to borrow, or to realize on their property. When they do, the funds of the savers come into action, either by supplying the money needed to make the loans, or purchasing property such as the impoverishing[9] owners can not hold.

It is in this manner that "Excess" Savings, (see page 38) the kind of savings characteristic of times of depression, are invested. The savers, or those acting for them, will not employ their funds so as to create new wealth or productive capital, but will simply confine themselves to buying capital goods (fixed property, securities, etc.) already in existence. The savings funds re-enter the general circulation of industry and trade not by the act of investment, but by the expenditures of the impoverishing[9] borrowers and sellers, who expend the money to meet their living expenses or their losses in business. No working forces, therefore, will be called into action, by the act of investment, under such circumstances. *And if so, the* *original minus of demand, caused by the act of saving, is not compensated for by the act of investment.**

* * * * * * * * *

All economists agree that the saving activity will cause a minus of demand unless this minus be counterbalanced by the act of investment. And inasmuch as practically all savings funds *are* invested (otherwise they would accumulate in the money market) the economists concluded that such counteraction always does take place, no matter what the particular form of investment. We have shown, however, that this is the case only if the savings are invested in the Capitalistic Form, not if in the Impairing Form. The latter form will, quite automatically, become operative as soon as the opportunities for Capitalistic Investment grow scarce. Whenever they do, the saving process changes its character. Its inherent pernicious tendency will no longer be checked, and the savers' everlasting endeavors to increase the supply and reduce the demand will no longer be restrained from becoming effective---resulting in that disparity between demand and supply which we call depression.

Here we encounter the factor which introduces the minus of demand into our business organization as a positive, definite and unmistakable element—the long-sought-for cause of the chronic disparity between demand and supply, and the true cause of depressions.

* * * * * * * * *

I have so far, in this treatise, spoken of the "Impairing Form of Investment"; more properly it should be called the "Impairing Form of Saving." Though the manner of investment decides whether any harmful consequences take place or not, we should not lose sight of

* Further argument on this point will be found in Chapter 6, especially on pages 92, 96 and 118.

the fact that the source of the harmful tendency is to be found not in the investment but in the saving process. If the latter process could be brought under control, and, at times of depression, could be so circumscribed that Excess Savings—more properly called "Impair Savings" —would become impossible, i. e., that no savings could be made except such as can find investment either for Replacement purposes, (see page 36) or in the Capitalistic Form—in other words, if people could be compelled to expend for luxuries such part of their surplus income as could not find investment in the two ways just mentioned, the depression would at once be brought to an end. There would not then be an excess of working forces, since they would be absorbed in the production of luxuries (see page 108), so far as not employed in new constructions or for purposes of Replacement. Given the possibility of checking or controlling the people's saving activity so as to prevent the formation of "Impair Savings," a relaxation in new constructions, in fact their complete suspension, might take place, and still business would prosper, for there would be no disparity between the aggregate demand (for working forces) and the aggregate supply.

If, then, the suspension of new constructions does not necessarily lead to a depression, while the saving process, in its Impairing Form, most positively does so, it follows that the latter factor is the more powerful, the deciding one. As a matter of fact, this factor constitutes the ruling feature of all depressions.

* * * * * * * * *

A billion dollars of savings, applicable to the creation of new capital or wealth, but not so applied, can not find investment unless the non-savers of the community either become indebted or alienate property to the amount of a billion dollars. In Chapter III I have shown what factors come into play to compel the non-savers to part with their property or to run into debts—namely, falling off of the demand, unemployment, lack of income, and consequent impoverishment—all of these factors being brought into existence by the same primary factor: Impair Savings.

Thus a strange duplex action of the saving process can be observed whenever it assumes this "Impairing" form: on the one hand that process creates cash funds which, once accrued, will seek investment; on the other hand it creates market conditions which enable those funds *to find* investment—the bridge between Impair Savings on the one hand, and their investment on the other, being the impoverishment of the community. This specific duplex action, which constitutes the ruling feature of the "Impairing" form of the saving process, and which comes into play especially at seasons of depression, opens up a new field for investments strictly in proportion as the *regular* field of investment, the formation of new productive capital, narrows down.

* * * * * * * *

The Impairing Form of Investment is not solely confined to periods of depression. It pervades all times, varying in intensity, however. It may be considered as the complement of the Capitalistic Form, inasmuch as the two forms, co-existing as they are, absorb between themselves all savings funds that are not needed for Replacements (see page 36). But the share of absorption between the two forms varies. At very prosperous seasons most of the savings will be invested in the Capitalistic Form, and only an insignificant share in the Impairing; at hard times, however, the proportion may be half and half. An intermediate proportion will prevail at seasons which are neither prosperous nor poor. In new and progressive countries, like the United States, the Capitalistic Form will predominate; in unprogressive countries, like China, the Impairing Form. The latter is also more pronounced in highly developed countries, where most of the available resources have already been capitalized and where, in consequence, we find the masses not so well employed as in the United States, occupying a lower standard of life in consequence. That the two forms of saving co-exist in our communities, is clearly shown by the results; we see on the one hand a constant increase of capital, due to the Capitalistic class of saving; on the other hand a chronic lack of demand, due to saving of the Impairing class.

The individual saver seldom has any means of knowing whether his funds belong in the one class or in the other; nor does he care to know, as in either case he can invest them. He may put them in a savings bank, or loan them out on mortgage, or buy a house, or securities, or other kind of property with them; but what finally becomes of the funds, after he has thus transferred them to others—whether they serve to increase the country's wealth or whether they do not, that is none of his business, and is, in most cases, beyond his control.

As a rule we may take it that such funds as the saver does not make use of himself, will always be invested in the Impairing Form, this being their natural and primary tendency, *unless* they be deflected from that course by being drawn into some capitalistic enterprise. Looking at the matter from this standpoint it becomes clear why savings, if not finding investment in the Capitalistic Form, will, quite automatically, find it in the Impairing Form.

* * * * * * * *

It should be well understood that the harm brought about by Impair Savings is of a temporary nature only; it ceases as soon as the savings funds re-enter the channels of industry and trade, which is the case whenever they are spent for purposes of consumption, and are thus turned into goods or services.

As it were, each individual case of saving, of the Impairing Form, brings with it its own sphere of ill effects, the latter terminating as soon as the funds are finally expended for consumptibles. As a general rule the process, from beginning to end, is short-lived, so far as each individual case is concerned. But the multitude of cases and their constant recurrence, in connection with the aggravation caused by the Multiplying Principle, produce those conditions which in their entirety manifest themselves in the shape of stagnation in trade, and in the consequent unemployment of a large part of the working forces.

How long it takes before the harmful action is terminated in each individual case, and how much scope the Multiplying Principle has had in the meantime, depends upon circumstances, which have been explained in the footnote on page 49.*

* In connection with the varying results traceable to the operation of the saving process in the different countries, a peculiar point of great practical importance should not be lost sight of. One would naturally conclude that if Impair Savings are the underlying cause of the disproportion between demand and supply, then, the greater the aggregate of Impair Savings, the greater the injury they bring about; as it were, Impair Savings aggregating three billions should be three times more harmful than an aggregate of one billion. This conclusion, however, is subject to important modifications.

For the sake of illustration let us imagine two provinces whose resources are being drained by the enemy, one of them having been subjected to forced contributions for a year or two, the other only for a short time. Naturally the contributions come in more freely from the latter province than from the former, whose resources are fairly exhausted. Suppose the proportion of the contributions be as 3 to 1. Now, if we were to take this proportion of 3 to 1 as a measure of the damage relatively sustained by the two provinces, we would be wrong, inasmuch as the exhausted province may suffer far more from the extortion of one million than the other from the loss of three millions. Just so with regard to the injury sustained by different countries from Impair Savings. In the United States the latter may aggregate one billion during a year of depression; in China, the country of permanent depression, they may not aggregate one-quarter of that sum, and still work far more mischief than the larger sum in the United States. To account for this, we have to bear in mind that Impair Savings necessitate a change of possession, the non-savers losing property in the same proportion as the savers acquire it, and evidently this change of possession can more readily be effected in a rich country, where there are many wealthy non-savers who have property to lose, than in a country like Chi-

Though the harmful action, brought about by the Impair Savings, ceases as soon as the savings are expended for commodities, it is important to remember that such expenditure can not take place before the damage is done.

* * * * * * * *

According to the views now prevailing on the subject, savings, as a rule, will benefit the community if invested, and will prove harmful only if hoarded. Looking at the matter in the light of our investigation, however, we find that savings are invested to a large extent in a manner which will not benefit the community, but impoverish it and will largely impede trade and business activity. Let us summarize the leading features of these various forms of the saving process, including the hoarding form (always keeping in mind that the difference between the several forms depends entirely upon the *manner of applying* the savings) as follows:

THE HOARDING FORM, where savings are not invested at all, but remain in the shape of idle cash funds, at least for a long time. This form is known to be highly injurious to business.

---

na, where poverty is the rule. And we further have to bear in mind, that until this change of possession is effected, the saved-up-funds will not re-enter their legitimate course in the channels of industry, trade and consumption (the Red Ring of the Chart), and in the meantime the "lack of demand" will multiply, unemployment will spread, and incomes will shrink amongst the producing classes.

The injury, therefore, which is brought about by Impair Savings cannot be gauged by the totals which they represent, but is dependent very much upon circumstances. As a general thing, the poorer a country, the more harm will they bring about, and the more will the harm be likely to assume a permanent character; the richer a country, the less harm. Within one and the same country, however, the damage done will more closely correspond to the aggregate of Impair Savings, though even here an exact ratio does not obtain; doubling the amount of Impair Savings will more than double, perhaps quadruple, the annihilation of income.

In a certain way we may liken the harm done by Impair Savings to that done by hoarding. An amount of $1,000, withdrawn from circulation and hoarded, is sure to bring with it more or less disturbance by engendering a diminution of the demand; but evidently to a far greater extent in a country like China where cash funds are quite scarce (and where their disappearance is more felt) than in the United States, where they are incomparably more abundant. What holds true of hoarding also holds true of Impair Savings, though in a lesser degree.

THE CAPITALISTIC FORM, where savings are invested in the creation of new wealth, principally such as consists of productive capital. Here the act of investment will turn the savings into income for those to whom the money goes, in the shape of payment for services rendered; which services may be rendered either in the construction of said capital, or in the production of the material for it. This form entails no lack of demand for working forces (though there is more or less *shifting* of the latter), but will rather *stimulate* the demand, and tend to increase production and to help business. It enriches the savers as well as the community, and is the basis of all accumulated wealth.

THE IMPAIRING FORM, where savings are invested not in the creation of new wealth but in the acquisition of property already existing; this in connection with the impoverishment[9] of the previous owners, and *the impoverishment being brought about by the very saving activity on the part of the savers.** This form of saving differs from the Hoarding Form inasmuch as the savings funds are not left idle for any length of time, but are seeking *and finding* investment. It differs from the Capitalistic Form inasmuch as it does not lead to the formation of new capital. It enriches the savers at the expense of the non-savers, making the latter lose as much property as the savers gain, but in addition making the community lose income to a much larger amount (see page 43). It tends to lessen the demand and thereby to impair business activity, though not to such an extent as the Hoarding Form does.

The three forms of saving enumerated above comprise only such savings funds as are available for the creation of additional wealth—the "Net Savings" of the Chart. Other savings are required for Replacements

---

* The above does not mean that if B, owing to impoverishment, has to sell his house to A, it must be specifically A's saving activity which made B poorer. His impoverishment is due to general market conditions, to the lack of demand brought about by the concurrent saving activity of a great number of individuals.

(see page 36), and for various minor purposes. The latter, however, do not cut much of a figure so their discussion need not come within the scope of our present inquiry.

* * * * * * * *

Apparently, depressions are due to the relaxation in new constructions, this being the cause most generally assumed in modern economics. The real cause, however, must be found in the fact that the saving activity changes its character—the Impairing Form of Saving, as just defined, prevailing to a much larger extent at times of depression.

There is only one remedy for depressions, and that is, The prevention of Impair Savings. To attain this end, two methods are imaginable—first, by creating unlimited opportunities for profitable investment in building up new productive capital, so that all savings, no matter to what extent they accrue, can find investment in the Capitalistic Form—which method, as explained on pages 62 to 64, would be impossible to follow out; second, by checking the saving activity, so as to limit the aggregate of savings to such a volume as can find investment either in the Capitalistic Form or in Replacements (see page 36), and thus prevent the very formation of an excess of savings. If we could bring the saving activity under control so as to allow it free scope only so long as savings funds can find ready investment in the creation of new wealth, but check it or impede it whenever the opportunities for such kind of investment become scarce—then we would have the means in our hands for preventing depressions. Whether a simple and practicable means can be found to attain this end—that is a question which it is not the purpose of this treatise to discuss.

CHAPTER VI.

PROS AND CONS.

THE primary cause of depressions has, in the previous chapter, been traced to the saving process. Many authors have, before this, arrived at the same conclusion and have insisted upon the existence of such a connection, without, however, succeeding *in proving* it. Their arguments were met by such forceful objections and counter-arguments that all efforts heretofore made to establish that connection, must be considered as failures. As matters now stand, the great majority of economists are inclined to look only at the bright side of the saving process, not at its dark side. The latter, viz., its Impairing Form, has so far remained unknown, and therefore beyond the reach of consideration. Just so with the Multiplying Principle, which is a sequence of that Impairing Form. These two factors known, and their existence fully established, the situation is changed, and the weak points of the above-mentioned counter-arguments and objections can readily be discerned. I shall, in the following pages, enumerate and discuss a number of the "objections" above referred to, and shall furthermore consider some additional ones which, though not taken from current literature, will readily present themselves, from the standpoint of the views now ruling, as bearing against the Impair-Savings Theory, and I will show where they are wrong.

OBJECTION NO. 1.--According to a well-established axiom every producer who is willing to sell brings a demand into the market equalling the value of the goods he offers; for instance, if he offers to sell a hundred dollars' worth of wheat, he does so with the intention of buying a hundred dollars' worth of other goods with the proceeds, which would mean a demand to that extent. This demand asserts itself not only where he expends the money in the usual manner, i. e., buying commodities, but also if he saves it and invests it. The investment, no matter in what shape it takes place, means buying something or other, and therefore means demand. Hence, the view that there should be a shortage of the demand whenever the investment assumes a certain form (the Impairing Form), contravenes the above-mentioned well-established axiom.

REPLY.—A demand of some kind may spring up, due to the investment; but this need not necessarily be a demand for working forces—and it is this point which decides whether there will be unemployment, and eventually depression in trade or not.

Most economists do not admit this distinction and they hold that the demand, irrespective of the shape it assumes, will in some way or other lead to the employment of working forces[6]. Let us take some examples to see whether this view will always agree with the facts.

Suppose that the man who realized the $100 from the sale of wheat expends the money in the purchase of commodities. Then the latter will be reproduced, either in the same shape or in some other shape, and this reproduction will call one hundred dollars' worth of working forces into activity. Such kind of demand, therefore, which calls for commodities, is practically identical with a demand for working forces.

Suppose that instead of buying commodities the man saves and invests the $100, applying it towards the building of a house. This would likewise give employment to working forces, no matter whether the money be paid out for wages or in the production of building material. So the demand ensuing would also be of the desirable kind.

But if the investment does not take the shape of new constructions or extensions or improvements, and does not lead to some enterprise that will set working forces in motion, and is not absorbed in renewals or repairs—in other words, if the investment takes place in that particular shape which is peculiar to periods of depression—can we still assert that the investment of the $100 will create a demand for one hundred dollars' worth of working forces? If it does, the manner in which this is effected should be explained; but that has never been done by our economists.

That a demand finally springs up, such as will convert the savings funds into goods, remains undisputed. But let us consider the conditions under which it arises.

In the regular course of business each individual's demand (i. e., the final demand, either on his part or on the part of his family, for purposes of consumption), depends upon his income—from wages, profits or whatever source. And the extent of his income practically represents the potentiality of his purchasing power or demand. Thus, the wheat-grower referred to above brings a hundred dollars' worth of demand upon the market only because he has earned that much from the sale of the wheat. And such earning power must be regarded, from an economic standpoint, as the legitimate source of all demand. But is it also the source of the demand where Impair Savings intervene? No. Here the individual, as has been shown in Chapter III, does not earn the $100 which he expends for commodities. The demand which he brings upon the market does not originate from his income but from dire necessity, from the fact that he needs food, and clothing, and shelter, in order to live. The demand arising from this necessity exists quite irrespective of his income, and irrespective of the amount of Impair Savings accruing in somebody's hands. It would therefore be wrong to assume that the investment of these savings funds originates the demand.

Where the savings funds, when being invested, come to the receivers in the shape of income, they create a demand for working forces, the extent of this demand being dependent strictly upon the amount of the savings funds. When invested in the Impairing Form, however, the act of investment does not create such a demand. There is a demand for commodities, but it is not caused by the investment. Though the funds finally come to be expended for commodities, the money comes to the receivers not in the shape of income, but through alienation of property or by borrowing—over the bridge of their own impoverishment.

OBJECTION NO. 2.—The argument given in the pages just preceding does not prove a minus of demand to result from the saving activity, in its so-called "Impairing Form." It is a well known fact that savings funds, say $100, will, in the course of their investment, be finally expended for commodities; then they will call not only for goods but also for working forces (to reproduce these goods), and this represents a demand for $100 which offsets the original shortage of demand engendered by the saving activity,—no matter how the $100 comes to those who buy the commodities, whether in the shape of income or in some other way. If the original shortage is compensated for by a final plus, no minus can remain.

REPLY.—Much has been made of the fact that savings funds, no matter how they are invested, are finally transformed into goods. To test the merit of this contention, let us resolve the saving process into the three phases of which, as a matter of fact, it is composed, and note how these several phases vary in their influence upon the demand for working forces, according to whether the saving process assumes the Capitalistic Form or the Impairing—always bearing in mind that (as assumed above) a demand for commodities is equivalent to a demand for working forces[6].

THE THREE PHASES UNDER THE CAPITALISTIC FORM OF SAVING.

PHASE A—This comprises ***the saving activity as such.*** As is well understood, the act of saving will, primarily, tend to create a curtailment of the demand for working forces.

PHASE B—consists of ***the investment;*** either in some enterprise or in some new construction, say, in building a house. Here, the act of investing brings employment to working forces, and therewith income, thus counteracting the injurious tendency of Phase A.

PHASE C—consists of ***the transformation of the savings funds into goods.*** This takes place whenever the working forces to whom the money goes by the act of investment, expend that money for consumptibles and commodities.

THE THREE PHASES UNDER THE IMPAIRING FORM OF SAVING.

PHASE AA—*The saving activity as such;* which tends to throw working forces out of employment, the same as Phase A.

PHASE BB—*The investment;* this is effected by the purchase of capital[2] already existing, say, of a house, sold by the owner to meet his living expenses; or, eventually, by making a loan on the house. Here, the act of investment provides neither employment nor income for working forces; hence, the injurious tendency emanating from Phase AA is not counteracted.

PHASE CC—*The transformation of savings funds into goods;* this takes place whenever the loan, or the proceeds of the sale of the house (which, as premised, the owner had to dispose of under the stress of necessity) are being expended for commodities.

Comparing Phase B of the one form of saving with Phase BB of the other, we arrive at a striking contrast.

In the one case the act of investment will create a demand for working forces; in the other it will not.

While the savings funds are in both cases finally transformed into goods, a vital difference can be observed before this transformation takes place. A sum of $100, if invested under the one form of saving will, as it were, create two demands and will call for $200 worth of working forces, namely, $100 when the house in question is being built and again $100 when the receivers of this money (the builders of the house) expend it for commodities—while under the other form only one demand arises, viz., whenever the $100 is being spent for commodities.

Another point of difference, of highest importance, comes to light when we consider the following: While the investment, under the Capitalistic Form, gives rise to two demands for working forces, and while the combined process of saving and investing necessitates three demands (one for the work of the saver, one for the work of the builders, and one for the producers of the commodities called for under Phase C) we find, under the Impairing Form, only two demands (one for the work of the saver and one for the producers of the commodities called for under Phase CC); but these two demands require the participation of three distinct parties (working forces) before they can become effective: first, the saver; second, the borrower[10]; third, the producers of the commodities called for under Phase CC. Let us repeat, under the Capitalistic Form of the saving process (saving and investing combined) we find three sets of working forces and a demand for each of them; under the Impairing Form it likewise takes three sets of working forces (the saver, the borrower[10], and the producers of the commodities) before the savings funds can find their way back into the channels of production and trade—but of these three sets only two will find a demand for their services, the one set (the borrower) being condemned to idleness.

Where we have three sets of working forces and three demands, one for each, there is no occasion for a disturbance of the equilibrium betwen supply and demand. But a disturbance in the labor market is bound to follow where, as is the case under the Impairing Form of Saving, we have three sets of working forces and only two demands between them.

A disproportion in the labor market, with an undue preponderance of the supply, means unemployment for part of the working classes, lack of income, lack of purchasing power, lack of demand for commodities, and stagnation in business.

This disproportion can not be remedied by a different distribution of the working forces, or by removing part of them to a different country. The presence of these unemployed working forces, who consume (even though to a much reduced extent) without producing, is essential to furnish a contingent of borrowers[10] (as per Phase BB), this in order to bring the savings funds back into the channels of production and trade—otherwise the saving process would assume the Hoarding Form instead of the Impairing, and matters would be still worse. Though, as just stated, the consumptive power of the unemployed is much reduced, say, from 100 down to 20, the stepping in of the Multiplying Principle (page 43) increases their number so as to bring their combined borrowing power[10] up sufficiently to absorb all Impair Savings. Thus, while it may take one set of builders to absorb $100 of savings under the Capitalistic Form, in the shape of wages, it may take five sets of builders to absorb the $100 under the Impairing Form, in the shape of borrowings.

It should be well understood that the saving process will surely cause a dislocation between supply and demand unless employment be given to working forces *BY THE ACT OF INVESTING.* The mere fact that a demand for working forces will spring up *later on,* subsequent to the investment, is not sufficient.

The basic fact stated in "Objection No. 2" remains undisputed, namely: While the saving of $100 will primarily create a shortage of demand, there will be an equivalent plus of demand, even under the Impairing Form of Investment, when in the course of the investment the $100 is expended for commodities and transformed into goods. But our economists are wrong when concluding from this fact that the final plus will always compensate for the original minus. They overlook the possibility that, to obtain the final plus, it may take the participation of two sets of working forces, with a demand for the services of only one of these two sets, leaving the other set unemployed—as is so often the case at times of depression.

OBJECTION NO. 3.—While it is true that investments in new constructions will increase the demand for working forces above the normal, a hundred dollars thus invested giving rise to two demands of a hundred dollars each, as explained in the foregoing pages; and while it is true that if the investment takes place in a different way, it may call for only one hundred dollars' worth of working forces—the latter form of investment should not be construed as involving *a minus* of demand.

If we turn to ordinary business transactions in the line of production and trade, we find there, too, only one demand for an equivalent supply, a dollar's worth of the one for a dollar's worth of the other, and nobody will construe this one demand to constitute a minus of demand. Why, then, should we have a minus of demand in the case of the so-called Impairing Form of Investment, if admittedly every dollar so invested will be turned into goods and will call for a dollar's worth of working forces?

REPLY.—The above contention is to some extent identical with "Objection No. 2"; but the principle involved is so important, and my deductions differ so much from accepted views, that it may not be amiss to analyze the subject from various standpoints.

Above all we have to bear in mind that where the supply represents work done, or services rendered by working forces, the demand must involve a demand *for working forces,* and not merely for capital goods, otherwise it can not constitute an offset for the supply aforementioned. In order to ascertain how far a demand for working forces takes place under the Impairing Form of Investment, in contrast with the demand arising in ordinary business transactions, let us adopt a method similar to that used in bookkeeping, where they put the Debit on the one side and the corresponding Credit on the other; but instead of following up Debit and Credit let us ascertain *demand* and *supply,* putting the Demand for working forces in one column and the Supply thereof in another. By this method we are enabled to compare Demand and Supply under the two conditions above referred to, i. e., under the Impairing Form of saving and investing, as well as where no saving takes place at all. In making these comparisons a distinction should be drawn between what might be called "active" supply of working forces, i. e., where the latter are actually utilized—as against an "inactive" supply of working forces, where the latter, though standing ready to do the work, find no employment and are compelled to remain inoperative.

ACTIVE DEMAND FOR WORKING FORCES COMPARED WITH THE ACTIVE SUPPLY THEREOF.

FIRST.—UNDER ORDINARY BUSINESS CONDITIONS, COMPRISING ONLY PRODUCTION AND CONSUMPTION; ALL SAVING BEING EXCLUDED.

	Supply.	Demand.
A, a non-saver, who produces goods worth $100, and consumes goods worth $100, will supply active working forces to the amount of.....	$100	
and a demand for working forces to the amount of		$100
B, the individual (or group of individuals) who by his work earns the $100 expended by A, and in turn expends money for consumptibles to the like amount, will supply active working forces worth.......................	$100	
and a demand for working forces to the amount of		$100

From the above comparisons, which may be continued ad infinitum, it will readily be seen that so long as the saving process does not come into play there need be no minus or shortage of demand, and no dislocation between demand and supply, a dollar's worth of the one quite automatically giving rise to a dollar's worth of the other.

SECOND.—WORKING FORCES AS AFFECTED BY THE IMPAIRING FORM OF SAVING.

	Supply.	Demand.
A, a saver who produces and sells goods worth $100 (which amount, let us assume, he saves) will supply active working forces to the amount of	$100	
When investing the $100 saved as above he buys property already existing, but of working forces he buys....................		none
B, the seller of that property and receiver of the $100, does not get the money for services rendered, his services not being called for and remaining "inactive," so the "active" working forces he supplies amount to......	nothing	
When expending the money for consumptibles he brings into the market a demand for working forces amounting to......		$100

Contrasting the two tables given above, we find that while under the conditions set forth in Table No. 1, the supply always creates an equivalent demand, and consumption goes hand in hand with production, representing what is termed "productive consumption," Table No. 2 represents a certain class of "unproductive consumption"; B, the consumer, being forced to idleness, and his services remaining uncalled for, owing to the lack of demand in the market. This lack of demand is caused by the saving activity of A, in conjunction with that of many other individuals, as explained in Chapter III. While the saving activity of A may not *directly* lead to the forced idleness of B, it certainly causes a lack of demand somewhere and helps to create general market conditions which reflect upon B and under which he suffers.

On further comparing the two tables we find that the Impairing Form of Investment, as per Table No. 2, necessarily calls for two men (or groups of men), the one, A, supplying working forces (his own) to the community, but buying none from it; the other, B, buying working forces without supplying any. So, between these two parties (working forces) there is only one demand and one active supply. Quite different are the conditions set forth in Table No. 1. There we see that A not only supplies but also buys, and that B not only buys but also supplies. So we perceive two demands and two supplies on the part of these two men; whereas, under the conditions as per Table No. 2, only one supply and one demand can be found to appertain to the two men—which means unemployment on the part of B.

If, to make the comparison complete, we should extend this method of investigation to the Capitalistic Form of saving, our table would be changed as follows:

THIRD.—WORKING FORCES AS AFFECTED BY THE CAPITALISTIC FORM OF SAVING.

	Supply	Demand.
A, a saver, who produces and sells goods worth $100 (which amount he saves) will supply active working forces to the amount of......	$100	
When investing the money saved as above, say in building a house, he creates a demand for working forces to the amount of.		$100
B, the individual, or group of individuals, who are employed in building the house, bring an **active** supply of working forces into the market amounting to........................	$100	
When expending this money for consumptibles, they bring into the market a demand for working forces amounting to......		$100

Contrasting the outcome of the three tables we find that under the conditions represented by Tables No. 1 and 3 the supply always engenders an equivalent demand for working forces; while under the conditions covered by Table No. 2 it does not. In the latter case the savers sell their goods or their services to "others," but do not give "others" an opportunity to earn their money back. This class of saving brings upon the market a "lack of demand" as a tangible, definite and positive element—a fact which fully confutes the position taken in "Objection No. 3."

* * * * * * * *

To maintain an equilibrium between the supply of working forces and the demand therefor, each man (workingman, trader, capitalist &c.) who earns a dollar, i. e., who renders a dollar's worth of services to others, should buy a dollar's worth of services from others. It does not matter whether he buys direct, or through his family, or through third parties; nor does it matter whether he earns the dollar through handiwork, or brain work, in the shape of profits, or of interest, or in any other way, all of which should count the same as services rendered; the point being that where he earns a dollar from the community he should give "others" an opportunity to earn the dollar back. He does so if he buys commodities, or if he invests the dollar in some enterprise or construction, or if he saves it and puts it in the money market and subsequently somebody else invests it in some construction or enterprise. If not so invested, however, and if coming to those "others" in the manner described in Table No. 2, the dollar does not buy the services of these others by the act of investment. Then a disturbance of the equilibrium between the supply of working forces and the demand for them is bound to ensue.

OBJECTION NO. 4.—If depressions were due to the saving process, the countries most noted for the saving habits of their people, like France, should be the ones suffering most from depressions and unemployment. The reverse is true. As a matter of fact, we find France to be the country least subject to depressions and their attendant disturbances, and possessed of such a high degree of wealth as to confirm the commonly-accepted view that the most saving nations are the wealthiest.

REPLY (a).—The foregoing Objection is wrong in two respects: first, in losing sight of the difference between savings and Impair Savings—a large volume of the one being by no means identical with a large volume of the other; second, in assuming that the peoples of greatest saving propensities are the wealthiest.

It is not the extent of the saving activity and not the volume of surplus earnings which does the harm; all depends upon the manner of investment. In a country like the United States the surplus earnings accruing in the course of a year may be ten times greater than in a country like China, still there may be "too much saving" in the latter country, and in the former not enough to meet the requirements, i. e., not enough to supply the funds needed for new enterprises. Even in one and the same country the savings[1] may at one time be quite large and still not too large for the country's well-being; at another time they may be much smaller and nevertheless too large to be absorbed to good advantage. In the United States the present (1906) rate of Net Savings accruing, available for new enterprises, exceeds three billions annually; yet there would be room for additional savings funds if they could be had. Twelve years ago (1894) they may not have aggregated much more than half of that sum, yet they were too large to be absorbed in the Capitalistic Form, i. e., in the creation of new productive capital or wealth, so they were partly invested in the Impairing Form, and at once became harmful. I repeat, all depends upon the manner of investment as to whether the saving activity is beneficial or otherwise, not upon *the volume* of savings.

REPLY(b).—As to the alleged fact that the most saving nations are the wealthiest, we first have to define what is meant by a "saving nation," and in this connection have to make a sharp distinction between mere saving propensity on the one hand and actual saving, i. e., accumulating, on the other. Paradoxical as it may seem, nations of great accumulating power, like the United States, are not those of greatest saving propensity; and in turn, nations of great saving propensity, like China, are not the wealthiest. To demonstrate this let us take up various countries and examine the saving propensity as well as the accumulating power of the inhabitants.

Above all others, the French people are reputed for their saving habits, these being generally taken as the source of their great wealth. But are the French really as saving as is commonly assumed? Is not France the very birthplace of luxury? And is luxury consistent with saving? As a matter of fact we find that the wealthy classes in France are, by their very environments, required to live up to their means, much more so than in other countries, and in consequence there are but few of those huge individual accumulations of wealth, such as we see in England and in the United States, and these few are mostly in the hands of foreigners. Inasmuch as a nation's growth in capital and wealth depends largely upon the rich people's savings, and as these do not amount to a great deal in France, we find the aggregate of the country's internal wealth to be far from what should be expected when considering the people's alleged great saving power; and the annual increase of that aggregate is actually slower than in other leading nations.

This tendency to live up to their means is not nearly so conspicuous among the wealthy middle classes of France; but even here (and to some extent even among the lower classes) we find a greater disposition than in other European countries to keep up appearances, to dress well, to dine well, and to live in well-furnished homes. True, they nevertheless show a keen disposition to save; and though this disposition largely manifests itself in the shape of haggling to get the most value for the money (a trait not really identical with "accumulating"), still, the accumulation that does take place is principally due to the middle classes. On the whole, however, we have to conclude that the saving "propensity" is not such a marked characteristic of the French people as is generally assumed. Though they possess a fair share of this propensity, the latter is largely modified by their tendency towards luxury—the one disposition being the very opposite of the other.

While France's wealth is commonly attributed to the great saving power of the people, facts show that the country does not excel in either of the two forms of saving stated above—neither in saving propensity nor in actual accumulation of internal wealth.*

A much more pronounced saving propensity than exists in France is found in China; and if such a disposition of itself were conducive to wealth, China ought to be rich. As a matter of fact it is very poor. The saving

* As is well known, the recent expansion of France's wealth is represented largely by the acquisition of foreign values, not so much by domestic development; in other words, the surplus earnings of the people are to a great extent being invested in foreign securities, perhaps more so than in creating new productive property at home. It was a fortunate circumstance for the French people to find an outlet for their surplus earnings in such foreign investments—an outlet which would not have been possible without the intervention of a factor which will be explained on page 134. Had there been no other avenue for the investment of their surplus earnings except that afforded by home enterprise, France neither could have attained her enviable position in international finance, nor would her domestic prosperity be equal to what it is now.

going on in that country is not of a healthy kind. Such individual accumulations as are being made there, hardly ever find investment in new enterprises or in the increase of wealth, the opportunities for such kind of investment either not existing or not being made use of, and practically no new capital being built up except where European funds flow in. As a consequence the saving process has, long before this, assumed almost exclusively the Impairing Form*—aggravated, as it always is, by the cumulative effect of the Multiplying Principle; and as a result we find in China great poverty of the masses, unemployment, stagnation in trade, and a state of permanent depression.

The poverty of that country is generally attributed to the lack of labor-saving machinery and to the primitive state of production. The introduction of labor-saving machinery, however, is not encouraged where manual labor is abundant and exceedingly cheap. The abundance of labor is caused by unemployment and by the general lack of demand; this again, as heretofore explained, by the saving activity, if it assumes the Impairing (or eventually the Hoarding) Form—and either of these two forms is bound to come into play whenever the

* Economists generally hold that the saving process in that country is of the "hoarding" type. I dare say, however, that old hoards are being released and scattered in pretty much the same proportion as new hoards are forming, otherwise the money still left in circulation would be quickly absorbed and withdrawn. Now, if the aggregate of hoards does not increase, the scope of the hoarding process going on at present can be but limited.

On the other hand we have evidence proving the Impairing Form of saving to be quite general over there. If Li Hung Chang amassed a fortune of fifty million dollars; if this accumulation was not accompanied by an increase of the country's wealth; and if it did not consist of money hoards but of useful capital, it follows that his style of saving belonged to the Impairing, not to the hoarding type. He became rich at the expense of others—by means of a "Change of Possession" of property already existing.

Considering that the Capitalistic type of saving hardly exists there at all, and that the hoarding type is quite limited (for the reason just stated), and considering further that more or less saving is always going on there, it follows that the latter must be principally of the Impairing type—a fact which has been graphically demonstrated in Diagr. 3, which see.

savings do not meet an outlet in the Capital[2]-Producing Form. China's poverty, therefore, must be primarily attributed to the strong saving disposition of its people—thus bearing out the point we started with, that nations of great saving propensity are not the wealthiest. Were the people of China less inclined to save, or were the savings invested in new productive enterprises, there would be more business and less poverty.

In contrast with the example of China we find much less of a saving propensity in England and the United States, but on the other hand a far more rapid accumulation and a much higher standard of life. Here, the desire for a higher standard of life tends to create a greater demand on the part of the people; this demand stimulates production and therewith the formation of new productive capital; this, again, affords opportunities for the capitalistic investment of savings—which means real accumulation and increase of wealth. So the greater accumulating power practically depends upon a concurrent growth of the buying proclivity of the people. It would not exist, were this buying proclivity curtailed by a stronger saving propensity.

Were the degree of saving propensity really the deciding factor in the accumulation of wealth, then the Dutch should be richer than the French, but they are not; and they should accumulate wealth much faster than the Americans, but such is not the case.

From these comparisons it follows that the greatest degree of wealth is not found in conjunction with the highest degree of saving propensity, but that best results as to actual accumulation are attained by a judicious mixture of a saving disposition on the one hand and a desire for a better style of living on the other.

This desire for a more luxurious style of living, this toning down, as it were, of the saving activity, is the indispensable, and in reality the decisive factor required to ensure prosperous business conditions.*

OBJECTION NO. 5.—The Impair Savings Theory, in so far as it implies that not all of the savings can find useful investment, is contradicted by the fact that at all times cash funds will command interest in the open market. Business men would not offer interest if they had no need of the funds. The principal use, and practically the only use, which they make of such funds is to apply them, directly or indirectly, to purposes of production; and inasmuch as they can always apply them to that purpose, it follows that the opportunities for profitable investment in production, or in the capital-producing line, are practically unlimited. What is said here of cash funds in general will equally apply to such funds as accrue from savings. In other words, the fact that savings funds will always command interest goes to prove that there is no lack of opportunities for the investment of savings in the lines of production or in the creation of productive capital.

REPLY.—The above argument is based on the assumption that whenever interest is offered for the use of cash funds the borrower does this for the purpose of some profitable investment, and that such funds as accrue from savings are usually applied in that direction. As a matter of fact, however, loans are often negotiated under the pressure of straitened circumstances, the proceeds going to make good the impairments resulting from a shrinkage of income, especially at times of depression. If a business man "runs behind," he often has to resort

* It should be understood, however, that the "judicious mixture," referred to in the text, is not the only requirement necessary to ensure prosperous conditions. It may be jeopardized by an unhealthy condition of the foreign trade (see page 135). On the other hand, a favorable trade balance (see definition on page 135), such as obtains with the French (see page 134) and with the Dutch, will do much to alleviate the ill effects of an excessive saving propensity. The latter would have tended to make these peoples poorer, had they been confined to the home markets for the investment of their savings. The favorable trade balance, however, allowed them to partly invest their savings abroad, and thus made them all the more wealthy.

to borrowing to cover the deficiency. To class this kind of borrowing the same as borrowing for purposes of regular business or for purposes of enterprise and extension, would be improper.

In periods of depression a considerable proportion of the demand for cash funds comes from the source here indicated. As at such times the saving process largely assumes the Impairing Form, so that every $100 saved by the one entails a loss of income to "others" of perhaps $500, it is clear that among those "others" there will always be some quite eager to borrow the $100 accumulated by the saver, and willing to pay interest for the use of that money. And what is true of the individual amount of $100 is equally true of the grand total of all Impair Savings, even if they aggregate a billion dollars per annum. So, while the demand for cash funds may be there, this does not prove the funds to be wanted for purposes of enterprise or of new constructions, or of profitable investment.

If the mere fact that interest is being paid on loans were really indicative of business enterprise and progress, we should expect to find a very low rate of interest in an unprogressive country like China, where but little money is absorbed in enterprise and new constructions Actually, however, the rate of interest is very high there —as much as three per cent. per month not being un usual.

OBJECTION NO. 6.—In contradistinction to the view set forth in "Objection No. 5" many economists hold that at times of depression savings funds, and cash funds in general, do not find ready employment in new enterprises or in the lines of regular business. Their argument would run as follows: The palpable decline in the rate of interest clearly indicates an accumulation of idle cash funds, although the statistics of the banks and of other financial institutions may not reveal the full extent of the accumulations. If, as assumed in this treatise, cash funds (savings funds) can always find investment in the Impairing Form where they do not find it in the Capitalistic, there should be no accumulation in the money market and therefore no decline in the rate of interest.

REPLY.—It is true that savings funds if not finding investment in the Capitalistic Form will find it in the Impairing Form: *but not so readily.* The opportunities for investment are not so inviting. Nobody likes to lend money where it is to be used for covering up deficiencies. Even where property is for sale, like houses, factories, etc., and where it is offered at prices much below the normal, buyers hesitate to invest in the face of a stagnant or declining market. This hesitancy impresses itself upon the money market—we find a predilection for sound and safe investments, and a disposition to be satisfied with a low rate of interest rather than to run any risk.

At prosperous times a man may find investment for his funds in two ways, first, in new enterprises; second, in the purchase of property already existing. At times of depression the mode of investment first mentioned is greatly restricted and moneyed men will have to look chiefly to the other form; high-grade securities which yield a fixed return being especially in demand. This will tend to enhance the prices of such securities—meaning a fall in the rate of interest which the funds so invested will bring.

A falling rate of interest, therefore, does not confirm the conclusion arrived at by many economists as to its indicating the existence of huge idle cash funds in the money market in excess of the comparatively small amounts revealed by statistics.

OBJECTION NO. 7.—The demand for working forces should not be measured altogether by dollars and cents, as has been done on page 98, and all through this treatise. A thousand dollars expended for luxuries will not give rise to an equally large demand for working forces as $1,000 expended for common necessaries, the production of the latter generally requiring much more manual labor. So the gauge used for measuring the relations between demand and supply does not seem reliable.

REPLY.—**Inasmuch** as the demand for luxuries will of itself include, or at least lead to, a demand for common necessaries (as fully explained on page 69), the deductions drawn in the foregoing objection are not well founded.

On the whole it is not so important that the savings funds should, by the act of their investment, put the greatest possible number of men in activity, as that the funds be transformed from idle Surplus Funds into Active Money; in terms of the Chart: That they be transferred from the unproductive circulation of the black central field into the channels of industry and trade represented by the red ring. So long as they circulate in these channels, the purchases of the one mean income and business for the other, no matter whether the expenditures be made for luxuries or for necessaries.

OBJECTION NO. 8.—No attention has been paid, in this treatise, to an important economic principle intimately connected with the subject of demand and supply, namely, the fact that a demand for commodities primarily concerns and rewards *past* labor, such as was previously required in producing the commodities—whereas the author treats the subject of demand entirely in its bearing upon *future* production. As the future is wholly an outgrowth of the past, reliable conclusions can hardly be reached where the part played by the past is not considered.

REPLY.—Hundreds of volumes have been written to define the relations of present demand to past labor or enterprise. Such discussions may have their theoretical value but are of no practical avail and would throw no additional light on the "neglected point" considered in this treatise.

OBJECTION NO. 9.—The impoverishment of individuals and the consequent alienation of property has, in this treatise, been ascribed principally to the saving activity of "others." In most cases, however, the impoverishment, especially on the part of the wealthy, can be traced to personal causes. A man may run behind in his affairs, because he is hampered by ill-health, or by accidents, or because he lacks judgment in the management of his estate, or goes into losing enterprises, or lives too high, sacrificing his future well-being for the sake of temporary passions and enjoyments. Whenever the wealthy spend more than their income amounts to, their subsequent impoverishment is not due to the saving activity of others, but to what may properly be classed as squandering.

REPLY.—No doubt the impoverishment of wealthy individuals is often caused by their own doings. Were we to ascribe to this cause, however, the widespread impoverishment observable at times of depression, we might, with as much reason, also ascribe the high degree of unemployment, observable at such times, to individual causes. The fact that unemployment often can be traced to special circumstances of an individual character remains undisputed. A workingman may be disabled by sickness or accident, or he may not attend to his duties, or be quarrelsome, or negligent, or lazy, or intemperate, and owing to any of such reasons he may lose his employment. Nevertheless nobody will deny that if at times of dull business large numbers of men are thrown out of work, there are general and not individual causes at play Just so with the impoverishment of the wealthy. While sporadic cases of "running behind" may often be due to squandering, the far-reaching impoverishment observable at times of depression is evidently due to general, not to personal causes, and it would be improper to maintain that the losers come to grief entirely by their own fault.

* * * * * * * *

A sharp distinction, therefore, should be made concerning the two factors to which the impoverishment of individuals may be due, whether to Squandering, or to Impair Savings on the part of others. These two factors are very different in their nature and very different in their manner of action, and especially so in their bearing upon business and upon supply and demand; the one factor stimulating the demand without increasing the supply; the other stimulating the supply without increasing the demand. A spendthrift who wastes his estate in the purchase of commodities or personal services evidently brings more demand than supply into the market, and thus enlivens business. A saver brings in more supply than demand, primarily at least, as is well understood; and if subsequently his savings lead to Impair Investments, the act of investment brings no demand whatever upon the market, thus leaving an excess of the supply. Considering that this shortage of the demand, as well as the unemployment resulting therefrom, possesses an inherent tendency to multiply, as explained on page 43, and considering further that these two elements form the very essence of dull business and of depression, it is evident that the factor which ushers in these maleficent elements will hurt business and the welfare of the community far more than the squandering process will.

Much has been made of the point that a squanderer destroys wealth, inasmuch as he annihilates some of the country's capital and wastes the fruits of other people's labor—this being considered equally injurious to the country's welfare as the destruction of property by conflagration, floods, etc. We should bear in mind, however, that, while the loss of a house by fire will actually destroy the house, and reduce the country's wealth accordingly, the loss of the house by the act of squandering will do nothing of the kind; it will merely lead to a change of ownership, leaving the property itself intact. There may be some truth in the further assertion that the spendthrift wastes the fruits of other people's labor, inasmuch as he lavishly buys and consumes all sorts of commodities, especially luxuries. But the fact is, commodities are there *to be* consumed; i. e., to be destroyed or absorbed by use or consumption. A rich man, although living within his means, may use and consume commodities to a much larger extent than the spendthrift does, without being accused of wasting the fruits of other people's labor—and if *his* purchases do not constitute a waste of the country's wealth, why should those of the squanderer? Were there a dearth of commodities, and not enough in the market to meet the demand, then the wasteful consumption of the spendthrift (and in fact also of the rich) would leave others short of an adequate supply of such commodities as they really need; but where (under normal conditions) our markets are overflowing, and legions of workingmen stand ready to supply still more, if the demand existed, and where, on the other hand, the prodigality of the spendthrift helps to augment the demand for commodities and for workingmen, it seems entirely out of place to construe his lavishness as leading to an impairment of the country's wealth.

Of course, all this is true only within reasonable limits. If the squandering tendency should spread to a considerable extent, the money market may be unfavorably affected, such cash funds as are needed for enterprises and new constructions then being absorbed by dissipations, with a resultant dearth of cash capital. It may be difficult, however, to cite a single instance where a general dearth of cash funds was traceable to excessive squandering, and not to the great demand for purposes of enterprise and new constructions. So long as we find an ample supply of available cash funds (as is the case under normal conditions), the doings of the spendthrift will exercise no perceptible influence on the money market; and especially not at times of depression, when a lack of cash funds is hardly ever witnessed.

On general principles squandering is not commendable, for it hurts the individual concerned, and obviously it would be better that all citizens should live in comfortable circumstances rather than to have any of them reduced to poverty. But the contention that it destroyes wealth and wastes the fruits of other people's labor and that it depletes the money market to an undue extent—all this is based more upon fiction than upon facts.

OBJECTION NO. 10.—The author considers only two forms of investment, the Capitalistic and the Impairing; and maintains that savings, in order to find investment, are confined to one of these two forms. There are other ways, however, for employing savings or cash funds; for instance, by loaning them out to merchants, manufacturers, and others, who make use of them in the regular course of their business.

REPLY.—Let us follow up the various purposes for which a merchant may secure a loan, say of $1,000. First, he may intend to increase his business; then the loan would constitute an investment of the Capitalistic class. Second, he may have run behind, thus needing the money to make up for his losses; then the loan would constitute an investment of the Impairing class. Third, he may borrow the $1,000 to pay off another loan—in which case there has been no investment of cash funds at all, the $1,000 merely changing ownership when being paid over to cancel the old loan, thus remaining "investment-seeking" cash capital, though in the hands of a new owner. Fourth, he may need the money for temporary purposes, to bridge over the busy season—which would practically mean an increase of his business, the same as just considered under point No. 1, only of a temporary character. Whichever way we take it, we would find that the funds, if they really meet investment (and not merely shift ownership), will find it either in the Capitalistic or in the Impairing Form.

Just so with the alleged "other ways" of employing funds. So long as savings, or cash funds, are actually available for investment, and are not needed for Replacement purposes (represented by Lines 12, 13 and 14 of the Chart), they practically have only two avenues of investment before them, either the Capitalistic, indicated by Lines 15 and 16 of the Chart, or the Impairing, indicated by Line 17.

If needed for Replacement purposes (Lines 12, 13 and 14) they are not available for investment, and therefore would not fall within the range of "Objection No. 10."

OBJECTION NO. 11.—The amount of three billion dollars assumed in this treatise as representing our country's saving power, is much too large. While, as a rule, economists are cautious about naming a definite figure as representing, even conjecturally, a country's saving power, where there is so little material on which to base statistics, the majority of them will hardly feel inclined to admit more than one-half or one-quarter of that amount. The smaller its aggregate, the less its importance as an economic factor.

REPLY.—To some extent the data given by the census reports, indicating a steady increase of the country's wealth, should be a guide. Even though these reports may contain many errors and irregularities, they ought to be fairly correct on the average, and when comparing the successive reports with each other they agree well enough to merit confidence. And they undoubtedly point to the larger figure rather than to the smaller one, notwithstanding the fact that some of the increase represents mere appreciation in market value which has nothing to do with the saving process. Take, for instance, the decade from 1880 to 1890. This period certainly was not characterized by an inflation of market values. Still our country's wealth increased from 43 billion dollars in 1880 to 65 billions in 1890, showing an annual augmentation of over two billions, in the shape of actual, tangible property, no paper values included. This increment of wealth represents saving power to the like amount, excepting a few items which in their aggregate do not make up a large share of the total.* In 1890 the saving power was greater than in 1880, and hardly less than two billions per annum. For the boom period of 1905, 1906 and 1907 where the country's population, earning power and resources had wonderfully increased, the assumption of an amount like three billions annually does not seem out of place.

Another guide may be found in the extent of the annual issue of new securities. According to the compilations of the New York Journal of Commerce the total of the issues "authorized" for the first nine months of 1907 came to 1733 million dollars, and the total of the securities really issued during that period to 1025 millions—of which amount about one-third has been estimated to represent mere refunding or conversion operations, the remaining two-thirds constituting new capital such as

* These items principally consist of the following: first, the small appreciation in the market value of the property existing prior to 1880; second, the property built up with funds procured by the expansion of credit money, i. e., bank notes and bank credits (bank loans, "money in bank"), which funds do not represent savings; third, our borrowings abroad, represented by the growth of foreign indebtedness, the latter being no more than one billion at the utmost, for the whole decade. All of these items may not foot up more than a quarter of the total increase of tangible wealth reported by the census; perhaps not more than a sixth.

will absorb the funds of the money market and which must be supplied principally by the saving process. Figuring a full year instead of nine months, the total may come up to 900 millions.* This figure, large as it is, comprises only the issues of railroads and of industrial companies where each issue reaches a million dollars or more. Considering that the great majority of issues consist of amounts of less than a million; considering further that many other large corporation issues are made in the mining, navigation, banking and commercial lines—the said annual increase of nine hundred millions ought to swell considerably. The municipalities alone borrowed 200 millions from January to September, 1907. Bearing further in mind that all wealth in the United States owned by corporations has been estimated at 35 billions, or one-third of the country's aggregate, and knowing that not only corporate wealth is increasing but also that much larger share which is held by individuals, such as we find in the lines of agriculture, commerce and industry and in the possession of all employed persons—it seems proper to put down the present annual increase of capital and wealth at not less than four billion dollars, the bulk of this representing saving power.

American economists have not paid much attention to the great extent of our country's annual increment of capital. A prominent French economist, however, has estimated the latter to come to 2,000 or 2,500 million dollars per annum at the present time.† Suppose the saving

* For the full year of 1906 the railroads alone show an increase of capitalization (bonds, stocks, etc.) of about $800,000,000.

† Strange to say, while computing our country's annual capital requirement at 2,000 to 2,500 million dollars, that French economist puts the saving power at only 600 millions—holding that the balance must be procured from abroad. A strange idea, indeed, revealing a considerable degree of confusion as to the source of capital. If we had to borrow from 1,400 to 1,900 millions from Europe in a single year, where would we come to in course of time? Our total indebtedness to Europe, accumulating for the whole of the last century, has never been estimated higher than 2,500 millions!

Again, in what shape could such a huge amount of capital, a billion or more, be transferred from Europe to America? In the form

power were only that much. And suppose that at a time of depression one-third of that amount of savings were unable to find investment in the beneficent Capitalistic Form; as it were, that savings funds to the extent of 750 millions had to find investment in the Impairing Form; this would mean a direct impairment of income on the part of the people to the same extent. But by the stepping in of the Multiplying Principle, as explained on page 43, that amount may be augmented fivefold, or more, and thus may fully account for the extensive loss of income which we witness during depressions. Consequently, it would not prove much against my theory if instead of three billions, the country's annual saving

of merchandise—where statistics show the reverse, a large excess not of imports but of exports? Or in the form of money? I have shown on page 29 that either form is out of the question for effecting a transfer of such magnitude. Can it be done by the mere instrumentality of foreign exchange? According to prevailing views, yes. Suppose a New York banker, A, negotiates a loan of a million dollars with a bank in Paris; the latter telegraphs Morgan & Co. in New York to pay that amount to A; all this may be done within a few hours, and the transfer is apparently consummated.

But is it really consummated? Does not the payment merely represent part of the transaction? The mere shifting of funds from one New York banker to another New York banker—funds which were already in New York, either in the possession of Morgan or of Morgan's bank—that does not end the matter. The real transfer, from Paris to New York, will be made when Morgan and the Paris bank come to settle with each other. Then it turns out that unless foreign trade (understood in its broad sense, see page 135) leaves a balance to allow of such exchange transactions, the latter must be made good by means of gold shipments. To presume that over and above the limit drawn by the trade balance an amount like a billion dollars, or even the tenth part of it, can be transferred by mere exchange transactions would be preposterous.

Nor can new capital be procured by withdrawing it from old investments, though many believe it can. Suppose a man has invested his capital of $100,000 in building a factory and that he needs $10,000 additional cash for going into some new enterprise. Can he withdraw this money from his factory? No. He may mortgage the latter and thus raise the $10,000; then the new capital comes from the lender of the money, not from the factory. Or he may obtain the $10,000 out of the profits accruing from running it; in this case the money comes from his earnings and from what he saves out of the latter, but is not withdrawn from the capital originally invested in the factory.

As a matter of fact the cash capital required for building factories, railroads and other productive capital must be supplied by the saving process, excepting only the funds coming from the expansion of credit money and those derived from abroad (see footnote on page 115).

I have dwelt on these subjects at some length because considerable misconception seems to prevail as to the source of capital, not only on the part of the economist referred to, but of others as well.

power were only half that sum, or still less; and whether the Impair Savings come to a billion dollars or only to half that much. Either sum may be swelled to a very large total by the intervention of the Multiplying Principle, and may thus become an economic factor of sufficient importance to fully account for the phenomena which we witness in times of depression.

OBJECTION NO. 12.—The Impair Savings Theory is built up on two assumptions, first, that an excess of savings, over and above what the author styles "Capitalistic Savings," really exists; second, that these Excess Savings work injury to the community and thus become Impair Savings. The existence of such "Excess Savings" is open to question, so long as not substantiated by statistical material. Indeed, some economists believe that savings can almost always find investment in enterprise and new constructions and that, if at times of depression a lull in new constructions takes place, this is due to a lack of savings funds, not to a lack of opportunities for the "Capitalistic" kind of investment. If so, there could be no Excess Savings, and without these there can be no Impair Savings. Unless the existence of "Excess Savings" be fully established, the Impair Savings Theory has no real foundation.

REPLY.—Though it may be difficult to produce statistical material bearing on the subject, still the existence of Excess Savings can be proved by a chain of definite facts, as follows:

PROOF POINT 1.—At present, during the depression of 1908, many individuals and business firms are "running behind," expending more money for their current expenses than they earn; this "running behind" being caused, not by extravagance, but by a shrinkage of their income, and this shrinkage, in turn, being due to lack of employment resulting from general market conditions. For example, the Erie Railroad is "running behind" at the rate of much over a million dollars per annum, where before the panic it earned a surplus.

PROOF POINT 2.—Suppose these "Excess Expenditures" amount to a billion dollars (or any other sum) to which extent the said individuals or concerns—let us call them "The Impaired"—are getting poorer. If The Impaired consume a billion dollars' worth of commodities (or services) more than they produce, there must be others in the community, *savers*, who produce a billion dollars' worth of commodities in excess of what they consume. Either this, or the stock of commodities, kept on hand by the dealers, must run down; but as we had no accumulations of stock before the panic; and as at present (summer months of 1908) stocks everywhere have already run down to a minimum; any further shrinkage of the stock of commodities is practically impossible, so the fact remains that any further Excess Expenditures on the part of The Impaired indicate an equivalent amount of savings on the part of others. These savings represent what I have styled "Excess Savings."

PROOF POINT 3.—If The Impaired expend more money than they earn, how do they obtain the money?

It comes from the savers, and reaches them over the bridge of their own impoverishment, either in the shape of loans, or in payment for property which they have to alienate. Suppose some of The Impaired be workingmen, unemployed, who draw on their deposits in the savings bank; the latter, in order to procure the money, will have to sell some of its securities; and if the savers mentioned in Point 2 buy these securities, their savings funds come into possession of the unemployed workingmen—not in the shape of income but in payment for the securities alienated by them (or by their bank). If instead of the unemployed workingmen we consider the case of a business concern, say, the Erie Railroad, we find here, too, that the money the Railroad expends in excess of its income must come from others; presumably in the shape of loans; or by leaving accounts unpaid, which amounts to the same thing as contracting loans or debts.

Whether the billion dollars consumed in Excess Expenditures comes, directly or indirectly, from the billion of Excess Savings referred to in Point 2; or whether some of these savings funds stay in the money market, and other funds, already in the money market, go to The Impaired to pay for their Excess Expenditures, that is immaterial. Practically we are justified in saying that the billion of Excess Savings, accumulated by the savers, find their investment by providing for the Excess Expenditures of The Impaired—to whom the money goes, not in the shape of income, but over the bridge of their own impoverishment.

PROOF POINT 4.—The Excess Savings referred to in Point 2 (represented by Line 11C of the Chart, see also Diagram 2) are made in addition to the Capitalistic Savings (Line 11B) and are by no means identical with these. The latter, when invested, are expended for new constructions, and go to the working forces in the shape of income, for services rendered. They neither cause unemployment, nor do they go to the unemployed, or to The Impaired.

PROOF POINT 5.—If no Excess Savings were made; if that billion of dollars referred to in Point 2 were not accumulated in the shape of savings but were spent by the owners for luxuries, that billion would go to the working forces in the shape of income, for services rendered. Then the class of The Impaired would disappear. There would be no Excess Expenditures, due to general market conditions, for people would *earn* the money they expend. There would be an equilibrium between the demand for working forces and the supply thereof, and the depression would cease. It may not be apparent how an enlarged demand for luxuries will benefit all of the working forces, now wholly or partly idle; for instance, what advantage the Erie Railroad would derive therefrom. But the manufacturers of luxuries, when expending their earnings, would set *other* working forces in motion and this, owing to the well-known law of action and reaction, would react favorably upon all working forces in the community, including the Erie Railroad.

* * * * * * * *

Granting the fundamental point of the foregoing argument, namely, that Excess Expenditures (as defined in Proof Point 1) really exist at times of depression—a point which economists cannot reasonably dispute—the conclusion follows, with absolute certainty, that Excess Savings must be made concurrently, and to an equivalent extent, and these must be made in addition to the "Capitalistic" and the "Replacement" Savings. Excess Expenditures on the part of some, and Excess Savings on the part of others, go hand in hand, inseparably. And of these two elements the latter is the governing one, as shown in Proof Point 5. Without Excess Savings there would not be that "lack of demand" for working forces, nor would there be that forced "running behind" and impoverishment on the part of "others." The fact that Excess Savings lead to such injurious results, gives them their character as Impair Savings.

* * * * * * * *

In addition to the positive proof contained in the foregoing argument we could adduce a number of points of circumstantial evidence showing that the standpoint taken in Objection No. 12 is untenable. Let us cite some of these points, as follows:

CIRCUMSTANTIAL POINT 1.—Though some of our economists may share the view evolved in Objection 12, that there can never be any superfluity of savings, the great majority of them agree on the fact that more savings accrue at times of depression, than can find investment in enterprise and new constructions, *for the time being.* They arrived at this conclusion, not through mere bias, but after duly weighing the facts and circumstances bearing on the matter. In other words, they believe that class of savings to exist (temporarily at least) which I have called Excess Savings.

CIRCUMSTANTIAL POINT 2.—Not only at times of depression but also at normal times many investments are continually being made abroad, even where the security may not be of the best; for instance in the construction of railroads in China, Turkey, South America, Africa, etc., and, particularly on the part of the French, in the constant acquisition of foreign securities. This clearly reveals the fact that the opportunities for investment at home do not keep pace with the increment of cash funds and that the latter accrue faster than they can be absorbed and employed to advantage in the home market—thus demonstrating the existence of an excess of savings.

If, then, we find an excess of savings even at normal times, we should not doubt their presence at times of poor business, considering that then the opportunities for the Capitalistic Form of investment are becoming quite scarce.

CIRCUMSTANTIAL POINT 3.—In countries already well developed and teeming with all kinds of capital in the lines of industry, agriculture, transportation, etc., there should be more production of commodities, more income on the part of the citizens, and consequently more saving power than in new countries undergoing rapid development, where, owing to the less efficient means of production, the output of the working forces can not be so great. Nevertheless the greater saving power in the old country does not produce the results which we might expect in the shape of accumulation of tangible wealth, this being generally larger (per capita) in the new country. Thus we find, in the well-developed country, a higher degree of saving power coupled with a smaller aggregate of the fruits of saving—showing clearly that a part of the savings must find investment in a way not leading to the augmentation of wealth; in other words, that there must be an excess of savings—Impair Savings—due to the lack of opportunities for Capitalistic Investment.

CIRCUMSTANTIAL POINT 4.—If we were to be governed by the time-honored proverb, "By their fruits you shall know them," we would have to conclude that Impair Savings exist, because the conditions exist which they naturally will engender. If we know that Impair Savings will cause unemployment, lack of demand, and depression in trade, and if at times we find precisely these conditions to prevail without being able to trace them to any other source that will bear investigation, the existence of Impair Savings seems to be indubitably proven.

Let us recapitulate the conclusions arrived at in discussing the twelve "Objections" advanced in the foregoing pages.

FIRST.—Though the investment of savings funds will always engender a demand, this need not necessarily be a demand for working forces.

SECOND.—Though savings funds, in the course of their investment, will finally be expended in buying commodities, and though this will, in turn, create a demand for working forces, such demand may not compensate for the primary minus originated by the saving activity. A "lack of demand" is bound to result if *the act of investment* does not call for working forces.

THIRD.--While in the regular course of business production and consumption go hand in hand, the producer being also a consumer (he or his family), such is not the case where Impair Savings intervene. There, production and consumption are no longer united, and we find on the one hand working forces which produce without consuming, on the other hand such as, through enforced idleness, consume without producing.

FOURTH.—The nations of greatest saving propensity are not the wealthiest. Best results are attained by a proper mixture of saving propensity on the one hand and a disposition for the enjoyment of wealth on the other.

FIFTH.—The fact that savings funds (cash funds) can at all times find interest-bearing investment does not prove that by such investment the funds are absorbed in enterprise and new constructions, or in the promotion of the country's wealth.

SIXTH.—The decline of the interest rate, at times of depression, does not prove the existence of huge accumulations of idle cash funds.

SEVENTH.—The point raised by some authors that the demand for working forces should not only be measured by the amount of money involved, but also by the class of demand, whether for luxuries or for necessaries, does not seem to be well founded. The demand for luxuries will, indirectly, involve a demand for necessaries.

EIGHTH.—While the purchase of commodities (for purposes of consumption) will primarily reward *past* labor and enterprise, it will also stimulate future production. The latter function is by far the more important one and in fact the only one which determines the trend of business, whether brisk or dull.

NINTH.—The impoverishment of wealthy individuals frequently has its origin in general conditions beyond the individual's control, though usually ascribed to personal causes, squandering, etc. If really due to squandering, this does not inflict upon the community those baneful consequences which most authors speak of, and which are based upon erroneous suppositions—upon conditions which do not exist. As a rule the squanderer harms only himself, not the community.

TENTH.—It may seem that there are numerous ways of investing savings or cash funds outside of the Capitalistic Form (represented by enterprise and new constructions) and outside of the Impairing Form (described in this treatise); but there are practically none excepting only those indicated in the Chart by Lines 12, 13 and 14, see page 36.

ELEVENTH.—Whether our country's saving power amounts to something like three billions per annum, as assumed in this treatise, or to a much smaller amount, that does not give much of a guide for measuring the extent of the harm which possibly can be caused by the saving activity whenever it assumes the Impairing Form. Most of the harm is brought about by the intervention of the Multiplying Principle.

TWELFTH.—The fact that "Excess Savings" really exist—an assumption which forms the basis of my entire argument—though hardly susceptible of proof by direct statistical data, can be amply demonstrated by positive as well as by circumstantial evidence.

CHAPTER VII.

VARIOUS FACTORS AFFECTING PROSPERITY.

WHILE prosperity is bound to wane whenever the saving activity assumes the Impairing Form to any large extent, I do not wish to be understood as maintaining that this factor is the only one which may undermine prosperity. In reality the latter depends upon a number of factors, all of which must co-operate, and the absence of any one of them may cause business to languish. To go over the entire field and thoroughly investigate all these various factors would lead beyond the limits of this treatise. On the other hand, a crisis theory would hardly be regarded as complete, or even acceptable, if it ignored these factors altogether, and I therefore deem it approprate briefly to consider them.

THE MONEY SUPPLY,—The relation of this factor to economic disturbances has been dealt with to same extent in Chapter 1, but its importance justifies further consideration.

It does not seem that the kind of money, whether gold, silver or paper (even inconvertible paper) matters much in determining whether business conditions shall be prosperous or the reverse. The United States got along very well with inconvertible paper money in the decade preceding the panic year of 1873, better than England did with its gold standard; the merit of a sound monetary system apparently consisting chiefly in its commercial convenience. Much more important is a supply of money adequate to the country's needs, and it seems to be particularly the case that any drain which will reduce the supply below this requirement will work mischief. Such a drain may take place in various ways, and may be either an actual one, where the coin leaves the country or the circulation; or it may be a relative one, brought about by depreciation. At the time when Rome drained its dependencies in the shape of annual tributes, those dependencies withered. In modern times a tendency to drain the weaker countries of their cash is often brought about by foreign trade, but is met by the issue of inconvertible paper money, which renders the currency unfit for exportation—an expedient which, though not fully sufficient for maintaining that "adequate money supply" which constitutes one of the elements necessary to prosperous conditions, is certainly the next best thing to it.

There is a peculiar kind of drain, however, which has been steadily going on for the last ten years and which can not be met so easily as the one just mentioned. I mean *the depreciation* of money—a subject that has hardly received the attention it deserves. Not the depreciation that attaches to paper money, if inconvertible, or if issued to excess, but the depreciation of the sound money, of the gold itself, as indicated by the constant rise of all wages and prices. A certain total of the money supply may be adequate to carry on a country's business at a certain level of wages and prices, but not at a higher level, and if nevertheless the level rises, this would act practically the same as a drain on the money volume.

An artificial drain of this character goes on especially at times of prosperous business. At such times the workingmen, always struggling to obtain higher wages, are helped by the greater demand for labor, and they largely succeed in their endeavors. This means greater cost of production and this again higher prices of commodities

—a result which is still more aggravated by the action of the trusts in keeping up high prices and suppressing competition. Gradually the working classes find that the advantage gained from the higher wages is slipping away, owing to the increased cost of living, and to remedy this, they will again contend for higher wages. In consequence of this process more money is needed to carry on the country's trade and traffic, as has been strikingly illustrated by recent experience in the United States, where, in spite of the immense augmentation in the volume of money, there was so much of the latter absorbed in the regular channels of trade that a continuous paucity of cash funds was witnessed in the money market, so much so as to keep the latter constantly on the verge of a collapse. Under such conditions some circumstance, trivial in itself, may prove sufficient to shake confidence, and bring about the collapse, thus ushering in crisis and depression—which might have been staved off for years but for the disturbing influence of the enforced rise in wages and prices. A high protective tariff which prevents the leveling influence of foreign competition makes matters worse.

Here we arrive at a peculiar interplay of conflicting tendencies. On the one hand, prosperity tends to create an artificial drain of the money supply, inasmuch as it favors the rise of wages and prices and thus depreciates the money in circulation; on the other hand, this artificial drain tends to undo prosperity, or at least endanger its continuance, by injuriously affecting one of its essential conditions—an adequate money supply.

* * * * * * * *

History shows us a strange adaptation of a country's monetary requirements to its actual supply of money. In modern times, and especially in recent decades, the supply has increased enormously, but (except at times of depression) we do not find any part of it superfluous, all of it being absorbed in the circulation—apparently from the reason that wages and prices are always being pushed up to (or near) the limit which the money supply will permit. While this automatic adaptation of wages and prices to the country's total money volume exercises a stimulating influence on business activity so long as the supply keeps on increasing, it has the opposite effect if it diminishes, as we have seen in the case of Rome's provinces. In such an event wages and prices needs must adjust themselves to correspond with the shrinkage of the supply, and must come down to a lower level; but the transition process is a painful one, engendering severe struggles and bitter controversies before workingmen accept the lower wages and business men the lower prices. And as a rule it can not be accomplished without the intervention of depressions or economic disturbances.

Adjustments of this kind (whether of a depressing character if for the lower, or of a stimulating character if for the higher) have always gone on wherever the laws of supply and demand have had free scope so as to allow of proper competition. Within recent years, however, two new elements have sprung into prominence, tending to counteract the operation of natural forces—the unexpected power attained by the labor unions on the one hand and by industrial combinations (trusts, etc.) on the other—powers which have proved fully capable of enforcing a steady rise of wages and prices without the least concern as to whether the country's money supply is sufficient to meet the enlarged demands thereby imposed upon it. This unceasing and seemingly irresistible struggle for higher wages and prices which has gone on for a decade, and which, as stated, has been equivalent to an artificial drain upon the country's currency volume, tended to contravene one of the conditions essential to prosperity, namely, an adequate money supply. Of late years the latter has been largely augmented by artificial means, notably in the United States, in the shape of an expansion of bank money[5]. This expansion has been large enough to fully meet the increased demands made upon the money volume. But the expansion could not go on forever, inasmuch as it was breeding troubles of its own. Then the law asserted itself that the demand upon the money supply must keep within the limits of the money volume—a collapse ensued which made an end, for the time being, to the aggressions of labor unions and trusts and to their endeavors for higher wages and prices —a collapse which probably would not have taken place but for the doings of these two factors.

I repeat, an adequate money supply is one of the essentials of prosperity. Though business conditions will gradually adjust themselves to a change in the money volume, the process of transition means economic disturbance whenever the change takes place in the shape of a shrinkage of the volume--no matter whether the shrinkage is a positive one, in the form of a drain upon the gold supply, or an artificial one, in the form of depreciation, i. e. a diminution of the purchasing power of a gold dollar.

INDUSTRY.—Obviously, this is an essential of prosperous conditions. In a community of lazy negroes who shun work, we will not find business activity nor any wealth to speak of. But while industry is essential to prosperity, it will not of itself insure it, as is shown by the example of China, whose people are very industrious, but nevertheless very poor. It is well understood that in order to attain best results in the lines of industry and production it takes more than mere physical exertion, and that the latter must be supplemented by proper means of production, machines, factories, railroads, etc.

On the other hand, history tells us that even in olden times periods of prosperity have existed now and then in spite of the primitive means of production, whereas in modern times depressions are by no means uncommon, notwithstanding the multiplication of appliances designed to aid production.

In leading countries we find no lack of industry nor of the productive capital required to obtain best results from it; but we generally do find a lack of opportunities for industry to display its full powers, and to keep all working forces employed. At times, exceptional conditions may prevail where this rule does not hold true, as was recently the case in the United States and in Germany; but it is well understood that such exceptional conditions will not last and that sooner or later the high tension will relax. Then we will see normal conditions return: industry will suffer from the want of an active market, and part of the working forces, though willing to work, have to remain idle.

ENTERPRISE.—This element, too, constitutes one of the essentials of prosperity, though it is not quite so far-reaching in its influence as generally assumed. Many economists consider it to be the leader, the moving force in the march of progress and of business activity. As a matter of fact, however, it is as often the follower as the leader. All depends upon circumstances and conditions. Where these are favorable, and offer a reward to enterprise and new undertakings, the latter will not be lacking; where they are unfavorable, enterprise can not turn the tide, and. of itself, bring about prosperity. Let us cite some illustrations.

The building of a railroad through an unsettled territory in the United States, with the expectation of a subsequent influx of settlers, who will build cities and villages, till the ground and establish industries, may seem to be a clear case showing how enterprise leads and, of itself, brings business activity and prosperity into a wilderness. But does not enterprise, even here, follow circumstances and conditions, and would the railroad have been built unless the circumstances had been favorable enough to warrant it? In contrast herewith let us consider a case where the favorable conditions are doubtful. Let us suppose that some twenty or thirty years ago natives of China had contemplated the building of a railroad in their own country through a thickly-populated territory, where, from a European point of view, the success should have been immense—was it lack of enterprise which restrained them from going into such an undertaking? Hardly. They knew they would not succeed. They knew they would be sure to fall victims to the exactions of their corrupt officials and to the likin system which harries all traffic in China. Let us assume, as a third illustration, that a foreign power would give protection to the building of a railroad in China; then we will see enterprise come forward at once and capital flow in—simply because the conditions of success which were absent in the former case are now at hand.

We could cite many other instances to show that enterprise can thrive only where the conditions of success are pre-existent. In a new country like the United States, which offers many opportunities for new undertakings, unhampered by lawlessness or other drawbacks, there enterprise flourishes. In old countries, whose opportunities have largely been seized on already, the field for enterprise is much more restricted, consequently profitable openings are, to quite an extent, sought for abroad. Again, opportunities for enterprise become scarce during periods of depression; it is well known that at such times enterprise will not avail and is bound to lag.

Enterprise must be regarded as the antidote, or really

as the preventive, of Impair Savings, and therewith of depressions. On the other hand, the latter (Impair Savings) act also as a preventive of the former, the one tending to exclude the other. Where enterprise is sufficiently active to absorb all the savings of a country, there is no room for depressions. Where it does not absorb all of them and where, consequently, a portion will become Impair Savings, the latter will at once do their part to subdue enterprise—since they curtail consumption (as explained in Chapter 3), therewith production, therewith the demand for the means of production (factories, railroads, constructions of any kind), and therewith enterprise, the latter deriving its support principally from the demand for new constructions. Enterprise thus being compelled to slacken its pace, the formation of Impair Savings (i. e., of funds not used for new constructions) will grow in proportion, and this in turn will tend to check enterprise still more, eventually almost stifling it, as is so painfully evidenced by unprogressive countries like China and India.

Enterprise no doubt constitutes one of the factors essential for a country's prosperity, and the peoples most alert in this direction count among the wealthiest. But I repeat, it is not nearly so much of a primary factor as ordinarily supposed, being itself dependent upon the existence of favorable opportunities and, to a large extent, upon the absence of Impair Savings.

FOREIGN TRADE.—This, when in a healthy state, certainly constitutes one of the essentials of prosperous conditions. But on the other hand it harbors the possibility of peculiar complications. Though in the main beneficial to all parties concerned, it does not benefit all nations alike. In its highest conception foreign trade is considered a refined species of barter, and if it were nothing but that, no complications would result. But the foreign transactions do not always offset each other in the shape of goods or services; there are residual balances, and these may pile up from year to year, thus giving rise to the development of so-called debtor and creditor nations. The latter are always growing wealthy and evidently are getting the better end of the bargain. Debtor nations may likewise be benefited in spite of becoming indebted, provided they are thereby enabled to build up new productive capital at home, as is the case with newly settled countries. But where, as in the case of Russia, a country becomes indebted simply because it is too weak to successfully compete with foreign nations and because it is unable to hold its own in its trade with the outside world, there the complications referred to may actually set in, and may lead to poverty, to a weak economic condition, and to chronic financial embarrassment.

Such debtor countries gradually have to increase their exports as against their imports, the annual excess representing the tribute they pay to the outside world owing to their indebtedness—this as a sequence to the fact that at some period of the past their exports were not large enough to balance their foreign accounts.

A conspicuous example showing how the annual residual balances of foreign trade may pile up to an enormous amount in the course of many years, is given us by France, which is said to own more than 5 billion dollars' worth of foreign securities. To attribute this stupendous accumulation of credits entirely to the course of her foreign trade, may, at first sight, seem absurd, but is undoubtedly correct. How did France pay for those securities? For the one or the other of the individual loans she may have paid out the actual gold, but did her stock of gold, in the long run, become smaller thereby? Did not she manage to recover, from other nations, the gold so paid out? And could she recover this gold without giving goods or services in exchange for it? As a matter of fact, France paid for those foreign securities, not in cash, but in the shape of export goods or services. True, it also took a corresponding degree of saving activity on the part of the French people in order to accumulate the funds invested in those foreign credits, but these credits could never have been built up, and the saving activity would have been of no avail to that end, without the concurrence of the highly favorable trade balance. Suppose the latter were wanting, and French capitalists would nevertheless undertake to buy a billion dollars' worth of foreign securities; then they would have to send that much cash abroad, and the drain of gold would at once derange their home markets in a manner to make a continuance of such buying impossible.

The term "foreign trade" should be understood in its broad sense, covering not only the movement of goods, but all elements affecting a country's foreign account, such as ocean freight, expenditures of foreign tourists, interest accruing on foreign investments, etc. The two latter items form the chief source of France's favorable foreign balance—which, as is well known, does not manifest itself in the shape of a large surplus of exports over imports, but which nevertheless enables the French to continually augment their holdings of foreign securities.

While foreign trade represents the principal source of France's enviable financial condition, it also represents the source of the wretched condition of Russia's finances. This country has become heavily indebted to the outside world, owing to the unfavorable state of her trade balances, and as a sequence to this indebtedness she is subjected to a constant drain upon her resources, which impoverishes her in the same proportion as it enriches other countries. Indebtedness is no less objectionable for a country than for an individual,* especially so where no values are created to offset the debt. Can Russia's railroads, owned by the Government, be considered as partly offsetting her foreign debt, and to that extent justifying its creation? Hardly. Other European nations build their railroads out of their own resources, not with foreign funds.

Not only will foreign trade prove instrumental in making some countries tributary to others, but it may also interfere more or less with a country's economic conditions so far as home trade is concerned. On page 105 I have emphasized that those countries thrive best in which there obtains a proper mixture of saving propensity on the one hand and of spending propensity on the other; foreign trade, however, will to some extent disturb the working of this principle.

Let us conceive of an island commercially isolated, where the inhabitants are moderate savers but nevertheless fond of good living. If of industrious habits they would be wealthy, even though their means of production may not rank with ours. Business would prosper and the demand would be brisk. Should now the island be opened to foreign trade, followed by the influx of cheap foreign manufactures, the brisk home demand would readily absorb the latter, and without a corresponding outgo of domestic goods the island would soon become indebted to the outside world—a result which, as

* Some economists hold that where one country becomes indebted to another, this is practically a migration of capital, even where the debt originates from the importation of consumptibles which represent no capital and whose value is destroyed when they are consumed. For instance, a factory in the United States may be built with English capital, the latter coming over not in the shape of cash but of goods; such importation would relieve us from making the goods ourselves and would set our working forces free to work on the factory(?).

Such a transaction might be taken for a migration of capital, on the ground that we built up home capital sufficient to offset the foreign debt. In reality the transaction would merely prove that we were unable to hold our own in foreign trade and unable to pay for our imports with our exports.

stated, is as objectionable for a country as for an individual. Here we find that the inclination for good living, which among an industrious people ought to promote demand, and therewith production, becomes the means for impoverishing the community unless it is able to hold its own against the aggressions of foreign trade. As a consequence of such impoverishment the buying of foreign goods would soon meet a natural check, and the demand for home production would be disturbed from the very beginning.

A healthy condition of the foreign trade is therefore highly essential for ensuring prosperous conditions. Only where a country manages to hold its own in this respect, so as not to lose ground or become impoverished by foreign trade,—only there the proper mixture of saving and expending propensity will produce its beneficent results. And as a matter of fact we find that among the leading nations the evolution of foreign intercourse has taken such a turn that they are not (like Russia, Turkey and the South American States) left subject to a constant *drain* of their wealth, but on the contrary, they have shaped their foreign relations so that they derive a surplus income *at the expense of other countries*, which makes them all the wealthier.

Not only the economic conditions of a country may be affected by foreign trade, but also its money supply, as has already been pointed out in the early part of this chapter. All of which goes to show that a healthy state of the foreign trade is by no means an insignificant element in supporting business activity.

Outside of the four factors considered in the foregoing pages—industry, enterprise, an adequate money supply, a healthy state of the foreign trade—several others may be enumerated which likewise are important in securing a country's prosperity, such as: good laws; stability in the government; a wise fiscal system; a bountiful supply of productive capital; promptness in the investment of savings, etc., etc. But, strange to say, and here we arrive at the essential point of our discussion, all of these factors may co-exist in a country, and still prosperity may be lacking. England affords an example of this. We find all of the above factors well represented there, nevertheless periods of depression occur quite often—which goes to show that the presence of all of these several factors and the freest scope for their co-operation does not of itself suffice to banish those distressing spells of stagnant business. To accomplish this we have to keep that element out of our economic system which causes the discrepancy between supply and demand and which so far has escaped the attention of our economists—Impair Savings.

CHAPTER VIII.

RECENT UPS AND DOWNS OF PROSPERITY IN THE UNITED STATES.

IN the preceding chapter I have pointed out that the maintenance of prosperous conditions depends not only upon a healthy state of the saving activity but also upon the co-operation of various other factors—an adequate money supply; a favorable condition of foreign trade; industry; and enterprise. The latter two factors depend largely upon individual energy; and inasmuch as we generally find an abundance of this in our modern communities, we also find an abundance of industry and enterprise, the only limit being drawn by local conditions; so, if economic disturbances occur, the primary cause thereof should not be sought in a relaxation of those two factors. For instance, the panic of 1907 was not caused by any slowing down of industry or enterprise. Quite different is the situation with regard to the other two elements, foreign trade and the money supply. These do not depend so much upon individual energy, as upon a multiplicity of circumstances quite complex in their nature and hard to control, and though the figures and totals representing them may not vary much from year to year, these variations may in course of time effect considerable changes in a country's economic condition. To show how these important factors, saving activity, money supply, and foreign trade, will affect prosperity as changes in their status take place, a concrete example may be instructive, such as is supplied by the recent economic history of the United States. Let us review this, commencing as far back as 1893.

CAUSES OF THE PANIC OF 1893.

Previous to the panic year of 1893 two elements of disturbance had been at work for quite some time: first, our foreign trade (comprising the movement of merchandise and securities, ocean freights, interest, tourists' expenditures, etc.) had resulted in a growing indebtedness to Europe; second, the money supply had been artificially inflated by the annual injection of large amounts of silver currency. Now it is not true, though it has often been asserted, that business men and capitalists took fright at the silver inflation and on that account became chary of engaging in new enterprises, and that this fright caused the panic; for as a matter of fact the business world paid no attention whatever to the changing character of our currency previous to the catastrophe of 1893. Nevertheless, the inflation had something to do with the panic. It worked harm in an unsuspected manner. As explained on page 129, a gradually increasing supply of currency will not result in an accumulation of idle cash funds in the money market, but will usually find absorption in the channels of production and trade —prices and wages rising accordingly. Such rise of prices reacts upon foreign trade, making the home market a good one for foreigners to sell in but a poor one to buy in; and here we arrive at the cause of the unfavorable development of our foreign trade* and of the conse-

* It may seem that a rise of prices, if it took place, should have manifested itself by a rise of the "index figures" and that an unfavorable balance should have manifested itself by an excess of imports over exports; while statistics showed neither. Let us examine the reasons why the statistics did not reveal the facts.

The rise of prices, due to that inflation of the currency, was comparative rather than absolute. Prices in other countries were steadily declining (in compliance with the universal retrograde movement of prices which took place between 1873 and 1897), but with us the decline was largely checked by the inflation of the currency. Without this inflation all prices and wages would have been forced to a lower basis, the same as in Europe, and we then would have been in a better position to hold our own in foreign trade. But as it was, we had comparatively higher prices, due to the inflation, without higher index figures.

As to the statistics of foreign trade, they showed quite an ex-

quent growth of our foreign indebtedness which took place at that time.

This growth could not go on forever. For many years Europeans had been content to take American bonds and stocks and other titles to property, in payment for the annual dues accruing in their favor, but finally they showed a decided preference for cash, and the drain of funds which followed reduced our money markets to that precarious condition where any untoward occurrence may cause a collapse.

LEADING FEATURES OF THE PANIC OF 1893 AND OF THE SUBSEQUENT DEPRESSION.

An untoward event, of the nature just referred to, took place in the spring of 1893 when a gang of speculators made an onslaught on the stock market. Taking advantage of the weak situation, they had been making "short sales" of stocks to a large extent, and now raided the market, managing to depress prices by all sorts of devices in order to cover their "short sales" at low figures and thus reap large profits. One of the devices consisted in creating an artificial shortage of money, which largely helped to depress prices and to shake confidence. They even went so far as to negotiate large loans with the commercial banks, paying interest on these loans but leaving the funds unused, thus tying them up and keeping them out of the reach of others. In consequence the tightness of money became quite severe, spreading from the Stock Exchange to other lines of business, and from New York to all parts of the country, everywhere de-

cess of exports over imports, for the years preceding the panic year, and might therefore be construed as favorable. For the four years 1889 to 1893 the export surplus averaged $73,000,000 per annum. When considering, however, that our annual dues to Europe for interest, ocean freights, tourists' expenditures, came to not less than double that amount (according to the compilations of the New York Journal of Commerce) and possibly to more, it becomes clear that the seemingly favorable statistics of foreign trade did not reveal the true situation.

pressing market values and prices, engendering distrust as to what might follow, and causing a mad rush to realize on property before things would get worse.

The panic continued for several months before the general anxiety was allayed. After that the funds which had disappeared, owing to the prevailing distrust, came forth from their hiding-places, flowing into the commercial banks and causing a glut in the money market. Confidence evidently returned, but not prosperity. Large amounts of idle cash funds were on hand, ready for any profitable investment that might offer, but such opportunities had become exceedingly scarce. Enterprise seemed to be stifled. Ordinarily the field for enterprise and for investments must be found in the creation of new productive capital; like factories, etc.; but an extension of these pre-supposes an increased demand for their products, and this demand was lacking.

Why was it lacking? What caused the great falling off of the demand which took place at that time? It was brought about by that mysterious factor which so often has proved the scourge of mankind—the saving activity in its Impairing Form.

Previous to the panic the saving activity was of a different character, manifesting itself principally in the beneficent Captalistic Form, in the creation of new constructions and of additional wealth. This, its proper and desirable sphere of action, was closed to it by the panic, and at once it was changed from a source of good to a source of evil. Not finding investment any longer in new constructions (except to a limited extent), the savings funds found it in that peculiar manner where the act of investing does not bring with it a demand for working forces, and where the services of the latter are left uncalled for. If at that period all saving activity had ceased, and if the wealthy, instead of continuing to accumulate part of their income, had made larger expenditures for luxuries, a corresponding demand for working forces would have ensued and the depression would have ceased at once. The wealthy, however, did not pursue such a course; the saving activity went on—therefore the depression.

True, a cessation of the saving activity, though it would have done incalculable good, would not have relieved the trouble entirely, for the large foreign indebtedness still existed and Europe continued its demands for payment in cash, therewith causing a steady drain of our gold supply. This drain became so severe that at times it was doubtful as to whether the country's currency could be kept on a gold basis, the reduction to a silver basis seeming imminent. Only the strenuous efforts of the Government, aided by the support of a syndicate of bankers, saved the country from an exhaustion of its gold supply and from jeopardizing its gold standard.

The situation became still more complicated by the passage of a measure which, though commendable in itself, was of doubtful value under the circumstances, namely, the enactment of a law for reducing the tariff. The lowering of the duties certainly tended to facilitate imports without correspondingly stimulating exports—at least not for the time being—and the result of this tendency was fully disclosed by the statistics, inasmuch as the excess of exports over imports fell off at once, being only 75 million dollars in the first year under the new tariff, as against 237 millions in the preceding year. With all due respect for the principle of free trade, it should be admitted that the time chosen for enacting the new tariff was inopportune, rendering the country's trade balance so much the worse and correspondingly increasing the drain on our gold supply.

The foregoing will serve to show the far-reaching influence which foreign trade, and the status of the trade balance resulting therefrom, may exert on the monetary and economic conditions of a country. Ordinarily we find no monetary strain in a country where a depression prevails, that is, after the panic has subsided. Nor was such a strain experienced by us; nevertheless a constant anxiety existed about the money situation and about the question whether the Government would be able to maintain gold payments. This anxiety undoubtedly helped to intensify the general feeling of despondency and to accentuate the depression. The silver inflation alone would not have been sufficient to cause that drain of gold and that distrust in the stability of our monetary standard unless the adverse trade balance had co-operated with it. The silver of itself will not expel the gold. It does not do so in France, despite the great volume of silver circulating there. France's trade balance is favorable, so she practically has not to make any cash payments abroad, and there is no drain on her money supply. But with us the situation was different. We had to make large payments abroad in addition to what we paid in the shape of merchandise, and only gold was accepted in settlement, so our gold went out while the silver remained. It seemed as if the gold was expelled by the silver currency; in reality it was expelled by the adverse trade balance.

* * * * * * * *

It should be understood that the depression which follows a panic is not necessarily coupled with an adverse trade balance and with currency troubles. It is not so in England. There an adverse trade balance (i. e., an unfavorable balance of the *foreign account*) is practically unknown; nor is the currency a subject of concern except at times of acute panic; still, periods of depression have been quite frequent there. The example afforded by the United States in those memorable years from 1893 to 1897 has been chosen by me for the special purpose of illustrating a combination of those three important factors of disturbance: an adverse trade balance, an unfavorable monetary situation resulting therefrom, and last but not least, Impair Savings, the latter invariably constituting the governing element of all depressions.

THE RETURN OF PROSPERITY.

While it was the drift of our foreign trade which produced the various factors of disturbance witnessed during the depression of 1893 to 1897, it was a change in that drift which put an end to our troubles and opened the gates for the return of prosperity. This change was effected by two memorable events: the enactment of a new tariff law, and in the same year, 1897, an unusually bountiful harvest, coupled with poor crops in Europe, which enabled us to dispose of our large surplus at high prices. In consequence the excess of exports over imports rose to the phenomenal figure of $615,000,000 in the year 1897-98, part of which was paid for in cash; so the efflux of gold witnessed in the preceding years was changed into an influx, and the drain on our money supply came to an end. Owing to the new tariff, the imports of merchandise fell off as much as $150,000,000 in the year 1897-98, compared with the previous year, a fact which certainly tended to stimulate domestic production. The greater activity caused thereby as well as by the largely increased exports, resulted in swelling the people's income, this again added to their purchasing power and to the general demand, this again fostered production still more and therewith created an enlarged demand for the *means* of production, thus awakening a spirit of enterprise. Then the "Multiplying Principle" stepped in—enterprise and new constructions calling for additional working forces[6], and these in turn, when expending their income, giving rise to a more extended demand for commodities; in other words, the well-known principle of action and reaction was brought into play, which did the rest in boosting up business activity to the high-water mark. With the revival of enterprise that malignant factor, "Impair Savings," which for four years had clogged the wheels of prosperity, disappeared, the character of the saving process being transformed from the harmful to the beneficent type, from the Impairing to the Capitalistic Form.

The remarkably favorable trade balance recorded in the year 1897-98 fell off somewhat in the subsequent years, but nevertheless continued at a very high average; this for two reasons: first, the hard times from 1893 to 1897 had resulted in depressing all wages and prices owing to severe competition among working men and business men, thus enabling us to produce our wares at lower cost, so as to compete with Europe in many lines of manufacture; second, the protection afforded by the high tariff of 1897 which so largely excluded foreign goods from our markets stimulated home production and, strange to say, Europe acquiesced in this policy of exclusion and refrained from adopting retaliatory measures.

It has often been stated that if we want to sell to other nations we must buy from them, the one depending upon the other. There seem to be some flaws in that theory, however, for our own experience during that period demonstrates that we could manage to increase our sales at the same time that we reduced our purchases. True, this one-sided policy may not work in the long run, but it answered very well for the time being. It did not result in a shrinkage of exports; on the other hand, it broadened the home market for the sale of our own products, which, in addition to the energetic exploitation of our immense natural resources, afforded employment for our working forces to an extent never known before. Where all working forces find employment and where they are aided by the best possible means of production, prosperity evidently must be at its maximum.

COMPLICATIONS DUE TO FOREIGN TRADE.

In course of time, however, the one-sided policy referred to led to consequences which were not foreseen when enacting the high tariff of 1897. The latter harbors an element of mischief which has made itself felt more and more in recent years. It helps to raise all prices and wages, because it excludes the leveling influence of foreign competition. The rise of prices means a weakening of our position in international trade, rendering our market a better one for foreigners to sell in and a poorer one to buy in.

True, this tendency has not so far manifested itself in the shape of reducing our exports, which indeed are constantly growing; but the imports have been growing much faster (up to the fall of 1907), and in consequence we see a gradual shrinkage in the excess of exports over imports, and a waning of our favorable trade balance.

This shrinkage of the trade balance would do no harm and might be regarded by us with complacency were we situated as favorably in this regard as England, Germany or France*, or if only we could come out even in our international trade, without augmenting our foreign indebtedness. But the fact is we have already

* In those countries the trade balance is apparently on the wrong side, showing an excess of imports, which, however, they can very well afford to pay for out of the income derived from their foreign investments.

reached a stage where, despite the large balance of trade still running in our favor, the *balance of payments turns out against us*—a fact clearly evidenced by our appearance as persistent borrowers in the London money market.

What becomes of the large excess of our exports? Though not so large as in the years 1897 to 1901, it has still been averaging over 400 millions annually in recent years. Only a part of this amount is absorbed by interest on our foreign indebtedness, by ocean freights, expenditures of American tourists, etc. The remainder is probably absorbed by smuggling (especially of precious stones), undervaluations at the custom houses, and possibly by errors in gathering the statistics. Be this as it may, the fact remains that whenever our excess of exports falls much below 450 millions per annum, our borrowings in London (in the shape of finance bills and of contangoes on American securities) seem to increase.

Such being the present situation, and the probability looming up before us that our trade balances will diminish more rapidly hereafter, we may well ask the question, Where are we drifting?*

We might keep on borrowing from Europe, and might continue to place large bonded loans abroad (such as were recently negotiated in the French market by some of our prominent railroads, and even by the City of New York) and in this way meet the annual deficit growing out of our foreign trade. Such a policy, however, would only serve to bridge us over the present, and would render the final adjustment all the more distress-

* After the panic of 1907 set in, a remarkable change in the trade balance took place, exports increasing and imports diminishing —a change which averts any troubles from that source for the time being, and therefore is proving a considerable help towards the process of recuperation. It remains to be seen whether this favorable trade balance will last—at least to an extent that will prevent a recurrence of such an unfortunate state of our foreign account as we experienced in the period from 1893 to 1897.

ing, this aside from the fact that our position would become more precarious as we go along, since Europe might at any time cease to take our securities—an eventuality which is bound to happen sooner or later. Already the London bankers have at times been discriminating against our securities, charging as much as 8 and 9 per cent. on American contangoes.

It may be that history will repeat itself. The troubles we experienced in those hard years 1893 to 1897 resulted largely from our adverse trade balance and our growing foreign indebtedness. Precisely the same conditions seem to be developing at present, and they may lead to the same end—unless the drift of events takes a turn which changes the position.

* * * * * * * *

Thus we find that though our high protective tariff of 1897 effected an almost magical transformation from depression to prosperity, its after effects will breed trouble. It restricted imports for a time; on the other hand it helped to raise all wages and prices, thus gradually facilitating European competition in our markets despite the barrier erected by the high tariff. Had the moderate duties of 1894 remained in force, the change in our fortunes would have been less spectacular, but of a healthier character. Our surplus trade balance, though reduced to 75 millions in the first year under the low tariff of 1894, rose to 102 millions in the second and to 286 millions in the third, and most likely it would have kept on growing had the tariff been left undisturbed, perhaps to figures as large as those reached under the high tariff of 1897. At the same time the leveling influence of foreign competition would have prevented domestic prices and wages from rising to such figures as they did.

The sentiment in favor of lowering the tariff has of late become more pronounced. Possibly, however, a decided move in this direction may prove as inopportune as it was in 1894; it would, for a time at least, still further reduce our already diminishing trade balance.

THE RELATIVE SCARCITY OF CURRENCY.

In the foregoing pages I have dwelt at some length on the subject of foreign trade, and have pointed out that the harm arising from our unfavorable trade balance (or, more properly speaking, our unfavorable balance of payments) consists not so much of the annual tribute we have to pay to Europe in the shape of an excess of exports over imports—for which excess we get no returns—as of the possible reaction upon our monetary position. It should be well understood, however, that the latter does not depend entirely, nor even chiefly, upon the state of our foreign trade, but is influenced to a much greater extent by domestic factors—labor unions, trade combinations, and last but not least by the annual additions to the volume of "bank money[5]".

As to labor unions and trusts, I have mentioned on page 129 that they are ever trying to advance wages on the one hand and prices on the other, without in the least considering whether the country's money supply is adequate to stand the added strain imposed upon it by such advances. Obviously, the higher the average of wages and prices, the greater ought to be the money supply needed to transact the country's business. In a way, therefore, the efforts of those combinations resulted in a reduction of our country's money supply—not in its volume but in its buying power. In this sense the effect upon the money volume was almost the same as if part of it had been blotted out of existence.

To a large extent the lessened purchasing power of the currency in circulation was compensated for by additions to its volume. But these additions fell short of the increasing requirements of the country. The total circulation (outside the Treasury) rose from 1,640 millions in 1897 to 2,772 millions in 1907, an increase of about 1,100 millions. This additional supply of 1,100 millions had to meet a number of new demands upon the currency, caused by various factors, four of them paramount in importance: first, the growth of population; second, the extraordinary business activity; third, the rise of all wages and prices, calling for more currency in each individual transaction; fourth, the enlarged cash needs of the banks for reserve purposes. The absorption of money for the latter purpose has not received much attention on the part of economists, but its importance will be readily understood when we consider that out of the total circulation of about 2,700 millions (in July, 1907) there was over a billion locked up by the banks, leaving only 1,700 millions in actual hand-to-hand circulation. Of the 1,100 millions added to the currency between 1897 and 1907, over one-half was absorbed by the banks for reserve purposes, during the same period, leaving only the smaller portion to meet the other three demands mentioned above, those consequent upon the increase of population, of business activity, and of wages and prices. This proved insufficient for the requirements.

Nevertheless, we experienced no actual dearth of currency, at least not in the channels of production and trade; this on account of the great expansion in the volume of "bank money[5]", which to a certain extent took the place of currency, and is, in fact, coming more and more into use for some classes of payments where formerly currency was employed. This substitution, however, progresses but slowly, and on the whole the fact remains that for the payment of wages and for the purposes of the retail trade, currency is the thing needed.

Another reason which prevented an actual dearth of

currency in the channels of production and trade must be found in the fact that the bank money[5], of which an ample supply existed in the hands of business men, could readily be changed into cash, the banks being under compulsion to make such exchange whenever demanded, even where they encountered difficulty in procuring the necessary cash and often had to encroach upon their legal reserves in doing so. Business men, therefore, met no difficulty in procuring the currency they needed, so long as they commanded a supply of "money in bank." But a peculiar situation developed in consequence—on the one hand, monetary ease prevailing in the channels of production and trade, and on the other a constant dearth of funds on the part of the banks, who found it difficult to keep their legal reserves intact whenever their depositors, who needed the money for purposes of their current business, had to withdraw more of it than the banks could well afford to spare. In addition to frequent embarrassments from this source, they were exposed to a continuous pressure on the part of borrowers clamoring for loan accommodations far in excess of what the banks could grant—not so much for purposes of production and trade (demands which the banks generally considered as having precedence over others) as for purposes of permanent investment, in the shape of loans on bonds, stocks, mortgages, etc.

Owing to this double strain, the free funds of the commercial banks ran down in an alarming degree. The banks naturally extracted from the general circulation as much money as they were able to retain, so there was no more in circulation than actually needed. And whatever cash they could manage to retain was used by them, almost to the last dollar, for reserve purposes, as a basis for building up additional credits. The extent to which this was carried on may be inferred from certain figures given in Government reports, according to which the reserves held by the National Banks underwent the following change: in 1899 they formed about 30 per cent. of the total of the "deposits"; in 1906, only 20 per cent. This does not mean that the funds of the banks diminished in their sum total, which on the contrary rose considerably; but the structure of credits (and therewith of "deposits") soared to such a gigantic height that the banks' cash funds, despite their much larger aggregate, showed a smaller ratio when compared with the deposits.

The commercial banks managed to build up that structure of credit higher from year to year, notwithstanding the difficulty they met in gathering cash funds for reserve purposes, where the depositors withdrew the money about as fast as the banks tried to accumulate it. On the whole, however, the banks found themselves much hampered by this scarcity of cash (which, I repeat, was experienced by *them* only, not by the business man), otherwise the piling up of credits would have gone on still faster than it did. In this connection I may mention the fact that the New York banks, which are bound to keep a cash reserve of 25 per cent., have been unable, from 1904 to 1907, to increase their loans and therewith their deposits, despite the great demand for loan accommodation; such increase of loans as did take place in the United States being confined chiefly to country banks, where the reserve of actual cash, as fixed by law, need not exceed 6 per cent.

Owing to the great demand for cash capital and loans on the one hand and the dwindling of free loanable cash funds on the other, the condition of the money market grew more and more precarious. While the money supply certainly was ample to meet all reasonable demands, a growing disproportion developed between the two classes of the money supply, currency, and "bank money[5]". The volume of the latter had been swelling prodigiously, from 3,109 millions in 1897 to 9,602 millions in 1907. To maintain a proper proportion the currency should have been expanding in the same ratio, which, however, it did not do, and such increase of it as did take place was largely absorbed by the banks for reserve purposes, as explained further above. On account of this growing disproportion the bank money finally was unable to keep up its par value with the currency, a development which at once engendered general distrust and led to the crash.

UNHEALTHY BASIS OF THE BANK MONEY.

The prodigious growth of bank money[5] which took place during the period mentioned, forms a striking characteristic of the recent developments in the United States. That growth was due, as already stated, to the fact that the commercial banks (the creators of the bank money) did not confine their loans to the legitimate sphere, the discounting of commercial paper, but largely branched out into the field of permanent investment—making loans on bonds, stocks, mortgages, etc.* Of the total bank money (about nine billions in 1907) only the smaller part originates from loans made on commercial paper, the larger part having been issued on the basis of the above-mentioned securities. Nominally, it is true, the latter class of loans are not of a permanent nature, being generally put out "on call," or on short time, which gives them the appearance of being of a temporary character, especially so as the funds thus loaned out

* Such loans, as a rule, are not issued direct to the railroads or the industries needing the funds, yet they are indirectly. Suppose a railroad makes a bond issue with the help of a banker, the latter inviting the investing public to subscribe to the bonds; then the public as well as the banker will largely depend upon the banks to make advances on the bonds so issued. Thus the funds advanced by the banks really come to be used for permanent investment in the railroad.

by the banks constantly revert to them. In reality, however, the loans constitute permanent investments, for their aggregate does not diminish, expanding rather than contracting, and the maturing loans being paid off by making new ones, shifting them from one bank to the other and from one holder of the securities to the other. The money needed to pay them off for good (over five billions of investment loans and over nine billions of all classes) is not in existence—see footnote on page 17.

A peculiar characteristic of the bank loans, and one but little understood by economists, consists of the fact that they become money (bank money) after serving their primary purpose of furnishing cash capital to the borrower. The latter generally does not withdraw the amount of the credit in the shape of currency, but merely transfers the title to it to other persons, and each of these, in fact every man in the community, will treat such transfers of bank credit the same as payments in money. Thus the mere title, i. e., the mere right to draw money against the credit, *becomes money*, owing to the tacit understanding among business men to consider these rights as money. And the multiplication of these rights has, to precisely the same extent, augmented our money supply. The larger the aggregate of the loans of the commercial banks outstanding at any one time, the larger the aggregate of these rights, i. e. of bank money, and the larger the country's money volume.

I mention (though it is well understood) that a man who procures a loan from a bank generally borrows the funds to pay them out to others, while those others, who thus become the owners of the borrowed bank money, are not the borrowers.

It may seem unusual to count these bank credits as a part of the country's money supply. A business man, however, will count his "bank money" as cash on hand, just the same as the currency in his safe or in his till. This is true of the deposits in National banks, State banks and Trust banks, but does not apply to those in Savings banks (see footnote, page 20).

I repeat, two classes of loans have contributed to build up the enormous extension of bank money from 3,100 millions in 1897 to 9,600 millions in 1907; first, the loans issued by the commercial banks on the strength of commercial paper, backed by merchandise and to be redeemed out of the proceeds of the sale of the merchandise; second, loans issued on bonds, stocks, etc., the proceeds of which loans generally found their way into investments of a permanent character, i. e. in new constructions. These loans cannot be cancelled or reduced in their aggregate except by the tedious saving process. Without this latter class of loans that prodigious volume of bank money would not be half of what it is and would not have constituted that element of danger which finally led to the collapse.

EXCESSIVE VOLUME OF BANK MONEY, YET A DEARTH OF CASH CAPITAL.

It may seem contradictory that at a time where the volume of bank money[5] had attained such a gigantic size, representing so much "liquid capital" in the hands of business men, there should have been that extreme dearth of cash capital which was really witnessed. This seeming contradiction is partly explained by another peculiar characteristic of bank loans (likewise overlooked by most of our economists), namely, that they can be used for investment purposes only once. If their aggregate increases by one billion dollars, this amount of new credit money will supply the funds for building up new constructions of an equal value, *but no more.* Having once been used for that purpose, the bank loans become

"Business Money." Though originally entering the money market in the shape of cash capital, available for investment, they cease to be such as soon as they are invested. To make this clear let us suppose that a railroad needs funds in order to make some improvements, and issues bonds which its banker pledges with some commercial bank, the latter advancing the funds in the shape of bank credits. Let us further suppose that out of this credit (bank money) a sum of $1,000 be transferred to a builder. Does this amount represent loanable or investable cash capital in the hands of the builder? Certainly not. He needs that money to make payments for material and labor, only a fraction remaining for his profit. The $1,000 has become Business Money by being transferred to the builder, and when he transfers it to others it remains Business Money, the same as practically *all* bank loans. Every new owner needs it for use in his current business, and can not apply it to purposes of permanent investment except to the extent that he makes savings out of his income. Then, however, the funds employed in such investment would no longer be derived from bank credits, but from savings—evidencing the fact that bank credits, when once invested, can not be used again for investment purposes, and explaining why, in spite of that immense volume of nine billion dollars of bank money, all of which counts as cash, and originally appeared as cash capital in the money market, the latter was left bare.

In this connection I remind the reader of the sharp distinction we have to make between cash capital available for investment (funds which actually constitute the money market), and the cash funds which constitute the business men's working capital. These have already found investment, and though they may seemingly be idle for a time, they are needed by the owner for the purpose of carrying on his regular business, so he neither could afford to loan them out nor to invest them in some enterprise. Practically all of the nine billions of bank money falls within this second classification, very little of it representing cash capital available for investment.

CAUSES OF THE DEARTH OF CASH CAPITAL.

The abnormal scarcity of cash capital available for the demands of the money market, going hand in hand with the tremendous growth of cash funds in the shape of bank money—seemingly a paradoxical combination—presents one of the most conspicuous features of the recent economic history of the United States. What was the reason of the constant tightness of the money market and of that extreme dearth of cash capital in the years preceding the panic of 1907? We can conceive of two causes; either the demand for cash capital was excessive, or the annual supply of new cash capital was too small. Some economists prefer the latter explanation. They speak of extravagance on the part of the people, of too much luxury and good living, and of the consequent lack of saving power; too much of the people's income being spent, too little saved. As a matter of fact, however, there was never more saving and accumulating going on than in the years preceding the collapse.

Let us take a glance at the Chart. It represents the money market in the shape of the Black Central Field, and it shows the two sources whence the funds come to build up the money market: first, the red lines 10 and 11, standing for savings or surplus earnings, of a net aggregate of perhaps 3 or 4 billions per annum (see page 115); second, the red-and-black line 18, standing for *the augmentation* of bank money, which for the five years 1902 to 1907 averaged about 600 millions per annum. Never before, in the history of this or any other country, has the annual supply of cash capital attained such proportions—and the fact that cash capital of such magnitude actually did accrue, is evidenced by the visible consequences—by the concurrent increase of the country's tangible wealth to a like extent, shown by recent statistics. So the assumption referred to above, that the annual supply of new cash capital was too scant, proves incorrect. In fact it was quite large. But the demands for new capital were still larger. All of the funds derived from those two sources were readily absorbed for investment purposes, such as are represented in the Chart by lines 12, 14, 15A, 15B, 15C, and 16; i. e., in such ways as lead to the creation of new property and to the extension of the country's wealth.

If we find that the dearth in the money market prevailing in the years 1905, 1906 and 1907 must be ascribed, not to the scantiness of the stream of new cash capital flowing in every year, but to the abnormally great demand for cash capital, which far exceeded the supply, the question arises, What caused this abnormal demand?

It was intimately connected with the country's great prosperity.

And this prosperity hinged largely upon the abundance of opportunities* for enterprise and new constructions. The latter gave employment to working forces outside of those regularly engaged in production and trade; not only employment, but also income. This income meant increased purchasing power; this, increased demand for commodities; this, increased production of commodities; this, increased demand for *the means* of production, factories, railroads, etc., and this, again, ex-

* On page 161 it will be shown that the great prosperity resulted not only from the existence of abundant opportunities for enterprise, but also from an inflation of the bank money. The latter, however, could hardly have grown to the excessive extent stated on page 154 without the co-operation of the factor above-mentioned—the ample opportunities for investment.

tended still more the opportunities for profitable enterprise. This well-known inter-play of action and reaction was further stimulated by the rapid growth of population, which of itself extended the demand for commodities, therewith again enlarging the demand for the means of production, i. e., for new constructions. And all these new constructions, inasmuch as they called for more cash capital per annum than was accruing from the two sources mentioned—savings on the one hand and increase of credit money on the other—did their part in promoting that insatiable demand for more and more cash funds, stimulating the issue of bank loans, and therewith the excessive creation of bank money.

INFLATION AND DEPRECIATION.

In course of time the rapid inflation of the money volume—partly in the shape of coin and bank notes, but overwhelmingly in the shape of bank money[5]—developed mischief of a peculiar kind. It not only made possible the constant rise of wages and prices contended for by the labor unions and trusts, but harbored a distinct tendency of its own in the same direction, thus still further increasing wages and prices.

To explain the nature of this peculiar tendency let us assume, for the sake of illustration, that all working forces[6] in the United States earn 20 billion dollars per annum. When they expend this income, mostly for consumptibles and partly for the creation of permanent capital, they will bring a demand for working forces into the market which likewise amounts to 20 billions. Let us assume furthermore that this demand suffices to employ all available working forces of the country; also that the existing money supply is just sufficient to transact the country's business. Now suppose that the money volume were augmented by one billion dollars in the course of a year, in the shape of bank-money; what will be the consequence? This additional money, which enters the market as cash capital, can be used for new constructions and for commercial enterprise just the same as cash capital accruing from the saving process, see page 23, and the business men borrowing such cash funds from the banks will surely so use them—otherwise there would be no object in borrowing. If so applied, the money will be turned into income for working men and business men and will create a demand for working forces to the extent of one billion dollars, this in addition to the normal demand. The latter, according to our assumption, amounts to 20 billions, and absorbs all working forces of the country. Where the normal demand fully employs these, can the additional demand, due to the expenditure of the additional billion dollars, employ more of them—i. e., more working forces than there are? If not, will not the demand due to that additional expenditure simply result in raising wages and prices, without increasing the output?

The answer to this question may readily be found in the great delay in having orders filled and in the scarcity of labor which prevailed in the years preceding the collapse. Such scarcity, of itself, inevitably tends to raise wages, and therewith prices—which means a depreciation of the money supply. In other words, the great increase in our money volume was largely swallowed by depreciation; bearing out the statement made on page 129, that where the money volume expands, the country's monetary requirements will gradually adjust themselves to the larger volume.

INFLATION THE MOVING FACTOR.

In the foregoing sub-chapters several factors have been considered which played their part in shaping the peculiar economic development in the United States from 1897 to 1907—the great prosperity—the unusual demand for commodities as evidenced by the delay in having orders filled and by the scarcity of labor—the dearth of cash capital—the aggressions of labor unions and trusts —the growing depreciation of the money's purchasing power, resulting from the steady increase of wages and prices. The moving factor for all of these phenomena must be found in the unprecedented inflation of the bank money[5]. This factor should be held responsible for the excessive, over-strained business activity of that period, as well as for the subsequent collapse. Inflation was the cause of both.

Most of our economists are not inclined to admit the inflationary character of the expansion of the bank money and prefer to believe the great swelling of its volume to be harmless, on the plea of its being self-adjusting—expanding and shrinking according to the demands of trade; and the great expansion during the time of the boom simply being due to the great demand for purposes of trade. It escaped their attention that it was the inflation itself which created this demand.

How this was done has been explained on page 161. And in the several preceding sub-chapters I have already pointed out how most of the phenomena enumerated above originated from the inflation. Can we likewise attribute the dearth of cash capital to that cause? As it were, could the undue increase of the bank money cause a scarcity of the bank money?

It certainly can, paradoxical as it may seem. True, at first the increase will tend to *relieve* the strain on the money market. The increase of the total of the bank money by one billion will satisfy the demand for cash funds to an equivalent extent. But what will subsequently become of that billion of additional bank money?

Does it assume the shape of idle cash funds, to be a drug on the money market? No! It is needed by the borrower to make payments and is rapidly absorbed in new constructions. If so, it will increase the demand for working forces above the normal (see page 161); therewith the income of these working forces; therewith the demand for commodities on the part of the latter. This will over-stimulate the general demand. Then the means of production (factories, railroads, etc.) will be found insufficient to meet the unusual demand. In consequence more factories, more railroad facilities, and more means of production will be needed, which, in turn, means an increased demand for cash funds and for bank money—i. e., a demand for still more inflation. Thus the one inflation will engender another (at least in a rapidly developing country) and, if so, will tend more to strain than to relieve the money market—until the inevitable collapse makes an end to further inflation, for the time being.

I repeat, it may seem paradoxical that an artificial increase of the money volume should result in a scarcity of cash funds—but the same result has been observed at other periods of inflation. The creation of artificial money will (except in rare cases) stimulate the demand for commodities above the normal. This demand may seem quite healthy; and the increased production resulting therefrom may likewise seem quite healthy, inasmuch as it "merely follows the actual demand." Nevertheless it is the inflation which actuates this abnormal demand, and the latter will cease when inflation ceases

THE PANIC OF 1907.

As the primary cause of the collapse of 1907 we have to set down the overgrowth of the volume of bank money[6]; as secondary causes the various factors resulting from this overgrowth. The steady depreciation of the money had to work mischief sooner or later; the abnormal demand for cash capital, coupled with the constant tightness of the money market, created of itself a position impossible to maintain in the long run; and the growing volume of the bank money (see page 154), was bound finally to make itself felt in some way or other.

It was especially the latter factor—the excessive volume of bank money coupled with an inadequate volume of currency—and the growing disproportion between the two kinds of money, which precipitated the collapse.

As explained on page 151, of the total currency of 2,700 millions extant outside the Treasury in 1907, over one billion was tied up by the banks for reserve purposes; allowing for this, the two kinds of money compared as follows, in August, 1907:

Currency in hand-to-hand circulation..................	$1,700,000,000
Business men's "money in bank"......................	9,600,000,000

The fact that all of this bank money of over nine billions was redeemable in currency *on demand* emphasized the gravity of this disproportion. When a somewhat exceptional demand for redemption sprung up, in the shape of a run on a few New York banks, the proportionate scarcity of the currency disclosed itself in a sensational manner—the free funds of all of the New York banks combined, were readily absorbed and were found inadequate to meet this demand, so the banks were forced to stop redemption of the bank money[5], and had to suspend cash payments. Thereupon the distrust of bank money became universal, spreading over the whole country and giving rise to a premium as high as 4 and 5 per cent. on cash money as against bank money. Presently the whole complicated system of domestic exchange and of credit became clogged.

The further development of the panic and its gradual subsidence into a depression followed the usual course, well known to economists, so we need not go into the details.

THE SUBSEQUENT DEPRESSION.

During the early stages of the panic the opinion seemed general that the depression to ensue would be intense but short-lived. At present (July, 1908) nine months have passed with little or no improvement. What prevents the recovery?

In the course of this treatise I have repeatedly pointed out that the degree of prosperity bears a close relation to the extent of new constructions under way. While the progress of new constructions went on with great activity prior to the panic, it experienced a decided check when the disturbance set in—a fact painfully evidenced by the stagnation in the iron industry, the one preeminently concerned in new constructions. Owing to this check many of the Constructive Working Forces[7] were thrown out of employment, and this, in turn, reacted upon the working forces employed in the lines of production and trade (Multiplying Principle), causing considerable curtailment of income, of purchasing power and of general demand. In consequence of the falling off of this demand the incentive for undertaking new constructions disappeared, the productive capital already in existence (factories, railroads, etc.) proving more than sufficient to meet the reduced demand. As a result, that peculiar complication set in, common to all depressions: The entrepreneurs do not build because the people are backward in buying commodities; and the people cannot buy because the entrepreneurs do not build.

Instead of the dearth of cash capital so noticeable before the panic, we now see a plentiful supply of funds in the money market, with apparently no use for them.

Only in one line of enterprise are cash funds still in demand; namely, in the railroad industry; not so much for immediate requirements, which seem to be fully met by existing facilities, as to provide for the needs of the future. According to the opinion of a leading railroad man these will call for a billion dollars annually for a number of years to come, the capital invested in railroads having increased but little in the last five or ten years, although the traffic has grown enormously. If the money market's idle funds were applied in this direction, the revival of business would be much assisted. But a peculiar difficulty stands in the way, inasmuch as the railroads find it impossible to borrow at reasonable rates of interest, while, on the other hand, they are unwilling to issue long-term bonds at an excessive rate, such as they had to pay on the numerous temporary loans which they issued within the last two or three years. Thus, the money market presents the paradox of a superfluity of idle cash funds looking for employment without finding it, and, on the other hand, a great industry sorely in need of funds without being able to obtain them. Naturally, this state of affairs will not last much longer, and will come to an end as soon as investors realize that the world-wide strain for cash capital is relaxing, and that the outlook promises continued ease in the money markets for years to come.

While a revival of railway construction and improvement will do its share towards reviving business activity, we have to reckon with several other factors that will operate in the contrary direction. Let us enumerate some of them.

FIRST.—Wages and prices are expected to go lower, and while this expectation prevails, buyers are apt to hold aloof.

SECOND.—The annual expansion of the volume of bank money which was checked in consequence of the recent panic, is not likely to be resumed so long as the present abundant supply of idle cash funds continues. I have pointed out on page 161, how this expansion of the bank money has created an abnormal demand for labor and for working forces, just for the purpose of new constructions. This abnormal demand naturally ceases with the stoppage of the further inflation of bank money. If the demand, so far as it went beyond the normal, formerly absorbed say 3 per cent. of all working forces, this share of the working forces is now condemned to idleness. And owing to the stepping in of the Multiplying Principle this share of 3 per cent. may easily be increased to 10 per cent. or more.

THIRD.—The country's saving power has grown to a tremendous total per annum, especially on account of the vast fortunes that have been accumulating in individual hands. So long as savings and surplus earnings could find ready absorption in new constructions, i. e., in the Capitalistic Form of investment, well and good; but where this avenue of investment is largely closed, and where, in consequence, the savings must find an outlet in the harmful "Impairing Form" of investment[8], there, the greater the saving power, the greater will be the harm done, and the longer will it take to re-establish the equilibrium between the annual savings and the demand for them, i. e., the demand in the line of Capitalistic investment.

As against these three points which work in the wrong direction, we may hope that the many natural resources of the country, still unexploited, will, sooner or later, attract capital and enterprise, so that savings and surplus earnings can again find employment in their legitimate sphere. This would assure the return of prosperity; though hardly in the shape of that over-strained business activity which prevailed in the decade from 1897 to 1907.

WHAT OF THE FUTURE?

When business does revive, the question may arise, shall we not again experience the same troubles which led to the collapse of 1907? Have we any assurance against their recurrence?

Much was said in the years 1906 and 1907 about the danger threatening from the constant rise of wages and prices, which, if unchecked, would ultimately have to result in a collapse; and the argument was often heard that a set-back in business activity would really be desirable in that it would counteract the doings of labor unions and trusts, on whom was placed the chief responsibility in bringing about this rise. The setback has now taken place, and has indeed imposed a check upon that dangerous tendency. After a revival of business, however, labor unions and trusts will no doubt resume their activities, and their success will depend largely upon the extent to which business revives.

While their aggressions undoubtedly aroused much attention, and provoked a great deal of hostile agitation, designed to meet those aggressions, very little notice was taken of another equally important factor—the inflation of our money volume, which resulted from the enormous expansion of bank money[5]. As pointed out on page 161, this inflation not only made possible the constant rise of wages and prices, but harbored a distinct tendency of its own in the same direction, thus proving fully as harmful in its effects as the first-mentioned factor. To successfully combat the unhealthy depreciation of our country's money, evidenced by the rise of wages and prices, the agitation should have been directed not only against the labor unions and trusts but fully as much against the fearful inflation of the bank money. Few people, however, even recognized the existence of this factor. In fact, instead of devising means to restrain the inflation, most of the financial authorities unwittingly advocate additional facilites for expanding bank credits still more, inasmuch as they demand greater freedom in the issue of bank notes—a remedy which may be likened to giving liquor to an intoxicated man.

To guard against the excessive expansion of bank money and bank credits two expedients seem appropriate: first, all commercial banks (including the Trust Banks, so far as they create artificial money) should be held to keep a large gold reserve, say 25 per cent. of the amount of bank money[5]; second, nothing should be done to artificially augment the amount of cash in actual circulation—so as not to make it too easy for the banks to increase their reserves, and therewith increase their loans and the volume of bank money. If they simply could print bank notes on the strength of their "assets," putting these notes in circulation, and for every million so issued withdraw a million of gold from circulation, to be used for reserve purposes, the inflation might go on worse than before.

The proper method of dealing with an exceptional demand for cash funds and bank loans is the one everywhere adopted in Europe: An advance of the rate of interest. This would check, temporarily at least, many security issues, such as could not afford to pay the advanced rate, and thus reduce the demand on the money market. Most of the financial authorities in the United States, however, argue the other way, and hold it essential to maintain a uniformly low rate of interest, even when the demand for cash funds should become brisk. To attain this end they propose the creation of an elastic currency in the shape of bank notes, issuable at a low rate of taxation, the volume to expand or shrink according to the demands of the money market. They overlook the law of supply and demand. According to this law the natural sequence to an extraordinary demand should be: a rise of the interest rate.

Where this does not take place, and where an exceptional demand for cash funds is simply met by the manufacture of cheap money, namely, by the printing of low-taxed bank notes, another inflation of bank money is likely to follow as soon as business revives. Inflation, if once begun, harbors a certain tendency towards sustaining itself—the more there is of it, the more is wanted, see page 163.

True, the bank-note currency ought to be elastic enough to prevent the interest rate from going so high that there would be danger of a collapse of the money market. As it were, the increase of its volume should go hand in hand with the increase of the interest rate. For this purpose an "emergency currency" would answer, subjected to a high tax, say 6 per cent. Such a tax would allow the banks to issue emergency currency only when the market rate of interest rules considerably higher than 6 per cent., and the tax would drive the notes home, to be canceled, as soon as the interest rate would subside, i. e., as soon as the danger were over. (Also see page 187.)

* * * * * * * *

By following the latter suggestion we would have the means at hand, not only for guarding against a renewed collapse of the money market, but also for guarding against a resumption of the inflation of bank money, and therewith, indeed, we would have the factor under control which proved most instrumental in bringing about the collapse of 1907, and which, if not restrained, may prove equally dangerous in the future, after the revival of business. Of the three disturbing elements considered in the foregoing pages—labor unions, trusts, and inflation—the latter seems about the only one which is amenable to our control, all efforts to check the other two having so far proved futile. But by checking the one we will, in an indirect way, attain the means for exercising at least a partial check on the other two. It would hamper labor unions and trusts in two directions. In the first place, the general demand would become smaller because the factor now unduly swelling it, as pointed out on page 161, would disappear; in the second place, if labor unions and trusts should try, in spite of the smaller demand, to materially raise wages and prices, they would cause a comparative scarcity of money, and this of itself would tend to counteract such a rise.

Continuous inflation of the bank money will naturally lead to a collapse. Most of our financial authorities are unable to see that the collapse of 1907 was due to that cause. But another collapse may follow if after revival of business the inflation should be resumed in that reckless manner as before.

IN CONCLUSION.

In Chapters 1 to 6 I have established the theory that depressions are due to Impair Savings. In the present Chapter I have shown that the disturbances of 1893 and 1907 were brought about by causes of quite a different nature; the one of 1893 being distinctly traceable to the unhealthy condition of our foreign trade; the one of 1907 having its origin in monetary conditions. The present chapter, therefore, may seem to contradict the previous ones. But the apparent conflict will disappear when considering the point elucidated in Chapter 1: that, though Impair Savings always form the ruling and sustaining element of a depression after it once has set in, they may not constitute the factor which primarily caused the economic disturbance and ushered in the depression. An economic disturbance may be brought about whenever any one of the various factors essential for prosperity (see Chapter 7) is lacking; and a depression always accompanies the disturbance; but it takes Impair Savings to give continuity to the depression after the cause of the disturbance has ceased to operate.

Such is the case with our present situation (1908). The collapse which took place in the fall of 1907 can clearly be traced to the inflation of bank money and the concurrent strain on the money market. At present, however, these two adverse factors are no longer operative. So the causes which ushered in the depression have disappeared. As nevertheless the depression continues, a new factor must have stepped in to which that continuance is due. This new factor arose from a change in the character of the saving process. It consists of Impair Savings. Could this factor be removed, the depression would speedily come to an end.

In 1893 the situation was somewhat different, inasmuch as the unhealthy condition of our foreign trade, the cause which then inaugurated the panic, did not pass away after the latter had subsided. Owing to the unfavorable trade balance our gold supply had heavily been drawn upon previous to 1893 (see page 141), thus weakening our monetary position and making it easy for that clique of reckless financiers to engineer the raid on the stock market which presently developed into a panic. This unhealthy condition of the foreign trade extended over the whole period of the depression, and the latter was not relieved until, in 1897, our foreign trade took a decided turn for the better. So it may seem that the depression was entirely a matter of foreign trade, and in no way due to Impair Savings. As a matter of fact, however, the latter fully played their part. They set in as soon as the disturbance set in. Without them the panic never could have attained the dimensions which it reached; and without them the subsequent prolonged depression would not have existed—there would have been more buying of commodities, and less unemployment, and more of an equilibrium between demand and supply.

From whatever standpoint we approach the subject of depressions, we will find that as soon as we probe the matter to the bottom we inevitably encounter Impair Savings as their underlying cause. Other factors, such as described in this chapter, may engender more or less economic disturbance; but only when Impair Savings join (as they mostly do) will the disturbance assume that chronic, paralyzing form which we call depression.

On page 132 I have spoken of an antidote for Impair Savings, namely, enterprise. This is such a prominent factor in the United States, and the country offers so many opportunities allowing it to become effective, that the antidote ought to seem powerful enough to make the very formation of Impair Savings impossible. Yet at present, 1908, we have the fact before us that enterprise is largely paralyzed, and but little is being done to exploit our natural resources, so the antidote against Impair Savings has become ineffective. The latter have gained the upper hand. They destroy the equilibrium between demand and supply, and thus engender depression, at a time when all the elements of prosperity seem to be at hand.

* * * * * * * *

Have we any positive proof that Impair Savings are really going on during the present depression? I think we have—despite the fact that a large share of our saving power is constantly being absorbed by the issue of new securities, especially in the railroad line, to an extent quite unusual for times of depression. The savings so absorbed are turned to good advantage, and on this account the depression of 1908 is far less severe than the one of 1893. But not nearly all of the savings now made are thus absorbed for useful purposes; and the balance will create harm. Wherever we see people "running behind" and getting poorer, owing to general market conditions and to the lack of employment, there we see the effect of Impair Savings, thus giving us positive proof that Impair Savings exist—see page 120.

CHAPTER IX.

SUMMARY OF THE FOREGOING.

THE dual nature of the saving process, the radical change in its character under varying circumstances—stimulating business at one time, and depressing it at another—has so far not received due recognition on the part of economists. Practically only its bright side has been studied. The dark side, though often pointed out by authors of the present and of the past, has been largely argued away. So strong, indeed, is the sentiment of economists on this point, that where they find anyone who doubts the ultimate usefulness of the saving process, they will generally attribute such doubts to ignorance of one of the accepted axioms of economics. The sooner we discard the idea that so much saving means so much increase of the community's wealth, and the sooner we recognize that only a portion of the savings now made will benefit the commonwealth, the sooner will we be in a position to arrive at practical measures for doing away with depressions of trade.

A BRIEF REVIEW.

Let us recapitulate the leading points of the Depression theory developed in this book.

"Lack of demand" is the fundamental feature of all depressions. If we can learn the cause of the one, we know the cause of the other.

In the course of ordinary business the producer and seller of a dollar's worth of commodities will subsequently *buy* a dollar's worth of other commodities, either he or his family; so the supply should equal the demand, and there should be no "lack of demand."

A complication arises by the interference of the saving[1] process. The saver, though selling his own services or goods, does not care to buy those of others. And if he omits to do so, there must be a shortage of the demand. All economists agree in the opinion that the initial stage of the saving process tends to curtail the demand.

So long as the saver (or somebody else for him) promptly invests his savings or surplus earnings in the "Capitalistic" manner, i. e., in new constructions or in the creation of new wealth, that shortage of demand is fully compensated for. He will call for working forces[6] to engage in such new constructions, and his savings will be turned into income for these working forces. Then the inherent tendency of the saving process, to create a lack of demand, is fully counteracted. But if not so counteracted, that inherent tendency will become effective despite the fact that the savings become invested, and a shortage of the demand will follow—a shortage entirely due to the saving process. The latter then changes from the "Capitalistic" to the "Impairing" form. It serves no longer towards increasing the aggregate wealth of the country, but leads to a mere shifting of wealth, making the savers richer, *others poorer.*

This process has been demonstrated on page 40 by means of my "Basic Calculation." If the savers save up two billions in the course of a year, and become richer by that much, while the country's wealth or property increases only one billion, then they must have extracted the other billion from the non-savers, the latter becoming poorer to that extent. If the non-savers owned fifty billions at the beginning of the year, they will own only forty-nine billions at the end of it. So it was partly at their expense that the savers became richer. Without the saving process, this impoverishment of the non-savers would not have taken place.

How is this impoverishment effected? By lack of employment.

Suppose that in a year of prosperity, the aggregate savings amount to three billions, all of this being invested in new constructions, and becoming income for the Constructive Working Forces.[7] If that three billions of new constructions dwindles down, in a year of depression, to one billion, there will be two billion dollars' worth of "Constructive" Forces thrown out of employment.

Now let us further suppose that the individuals representing the unemployed part of the Constructive Forces had property which they could sell or borrow on, and that, by doing so, they were procuring the means for continuing their style of living and their expenditures precisely in the manner they were used to when fully employed; what character would the depression assume under such conditions?

The depression would then be confined strictly to the Constructive Forces, to the trades usually engaged in new constructions, and would in no way extend to the "Commodity" Forces[7]. The latter, representing probably 85 per cent. of the whole, would find just as much employment and just as much demand for their products as before, our assumption being that the Constructive Forces expend fully as much for commodities as formerly. Under such circumstances there would be no difficulty to recognize the true character of the change in the saving process. Instead of leading to an augmentation of the country's wealth in the shape of new constructions, it would merely lead to a "Change of Possession" of such property as already exists, the Constructive Forces losing property (or becoming indebted) to the extent of two billions a year, and the savers becoming richer by that much.

In the foregoing we assumed that the Constructive Forces, though not earning anything, would in no way restrict their purchases of commodities. In reality, however, they will economize, and very much so, even if owning property on which they could realize. They may reduce their consumption to one-quarter of what it was. In that case they would lessen their demand for commodities by a billion and a half. This lessening of the demand would entail a lessening of the production of commodities. This, again, would entail a corresponding unemployment among the Commodity Forces[7], and bring the total loss of income, due to unemployment, to three billions and a half. Nor will the loss stop there. Owing to the well-known process of action and reaction, unemployment will spread from one trade to another, multiply, as it were (Multiplying Principle) and bring up the loss of income to an amount much larger than the whole amount of the savings. The more the people try to meet the loss of income by economy and privation, and the more they cut down their expenditures, the more will the demand for commodities be lessened and the severer will be the stagnation in trade.

The Change of Possession (of property already existing) is inseparable from this, the Impairing Form of the saving process. The Change of Possession is enforced by means of unemployment and by the loss of income resulting therefrom. Among the unemployed (or only partly employed) there are many who own property. They need money to pay their living expenses. So they must either borrow or realize on what they own. Unemployment, therefore, and loss of income, form the whip which forces people to part with their property, therewith giving the savers an opportunity to invest their savings either in buying the property or in lending money on it. For every million of Impair Savings a million of properties or securities must go into the possession of the savers, otherwise the savings would accumulate in the shape of hoards, and matters would become still worse.

After the million has been thus invested, and the money been expended by the receivers, for commodities, the money returns into the channels of production and trade, and the chain of mischief caused by the saving of that individual million comes to an end.

* * * * * * * *

Ordinarily each individual member of the working forces is not only a producer, but also a consumer. Under the Impairing Form of saving or investing, however, demand and supply are no longer united in the same individual. Two individuals will no longer furnish two supplies and two demands, but only one supply and one demand; i.e., *for working forces;* the saver producing without consuming, and the consumer finding himself without the opportunity to produce, his services being left uncalled for.

Our economists have been arguing that inasmuch as all savings funds are finally turned into goods or services, thereby giving employment to working forces, the saving process can not give rise to a shortage of the demand, even at times of depression. They overlook the fact that before the saving funds are expended for goods or services, unemployment stands in between—unemployment caused directly by the saving activity, when assuming its Impairing Form.

I repeat, the saving activity always harbors the inherent tendency of causing unemployment and curtailing the demand. This tendency is fully counteracted whenever the savings are invested in new constructions or in the creation of additional wealth; but if not so counteracter, that tendency will become operative. The greater the amount of savings, and the smaller the proportion which finds investment in new constructions, the greater will be the harm inflicted upon the community. The harm so inflicted, invariably aggravated by the stepping in of the Multiplying Principle, will fully account for all the phenomena observed at a time of depression.

We cannot do away with depressions before we find means to restrict or eliminate the Impairing Form of the saving process.

THE THREE DEGREES OF BUSINESS ACTIVITY.

From the foregoing it follows that prosperity will be high or low, according to the character of the saving activity. In Chapter 8, however, a further factor has been referred to, namely, the inflation of the money volume, which likewise plays an important part in affecting the course of business. Accordingly, we may distinguish three degrees of business prosperity, as follows:

1.—HEALTHY BUSINESS.—Best results are attained when the annual savings[1] available for investment are neither larger nor smaller than the amount of cash capital required for new constructions[3]—always presuming, of course, that the other factors essential for prosperity (as enumerated in Chapter 7) are at hand. Then the saving process will not disturb the equilibrium between supply and demand, and there will be no lack of the latter. The aggregate of savings should not be too large, hardly over 10 or 12 per cent. of the people's aggregate income, in a new, progressive country; 5 per cent. in an old well developed country. In the latter case 95 per cent. of all working forces would be absorbed for purposes of production and distribution of commodities, and only 5 per cent. for new constructions. Then, if a lull in new constructions should take place, and part of the Constructive Forces[7] should be thrown out of employment, this would represent only a fraction of 5 per cent. of the aggregate of all working forces, so the reaction on the remaining 95 per cent. and on business in general would be but slight.

Such a healthy state of business is favored by a reasonably even distribution of wealth, such as obtains in France. The concentration of wealth in a few hands is not desirable, especially in old countries. It will unduly promote the saving process (see page 66). And though this may do no harm in a new country, like the United States, so long as wealth and population are rapidly expanding and all savings readily absorbed in new constructions, it will do harm when a lull in new constructions sets in. Then savings become Impair Savings; and the greater their volume, the more will the recovery of business be impeded.

2.—OVER-STRAINED BUSINESS.—This takes place whenever the supply of cash capital does not come from the saving process alone, but is largely supplemented by the creation of artificial money, by an inflation either of bank money[5] or of printed currency; especially so of the latter. In the United States it was principally the undue expansion of bank money (see page 161) which, in conjunction with the unusual extent of new constructions, imparted that over-strained character to business which marked the years preceding 1908. These new constructions caused more demand for working forces than could be had. Besides, they distorted the proportion between "Constructive" and "Commodity"[7] Working Forces, the former reaching a figure probably as high as 15 per cent. of the total, or more. When, in 1908, a depression followed the panic of 1907, there was still a fair demand for new constructions, but by far insufficient to absorb all of the Constructive Working Forces then in existence. And the surplus could not find employment among the Commodity Forces. These, constituting 85 per cent. of the aggregate, were fully capable of supplying the consumptibles needed for all, even at the time of the great demand during the boom, and are certainly so at present (1908), with the demand largely reduced.

Over-strained business, though imparting the impression of excessive prosperity so long as it lasts, is bound to come to an end sooner or later. It rests upon inflation, and this can not go on forever. When the process of inflation ceases, we find many unhealthy conditions to have developed: a superabundance of Constructive Forces, with no work for the greater part of them; wages unduly advanced, and therewith the general level of prices; foreign trade in a precarious condition, the home market having become a better one for foreigners to sell in and a poorer one to buy in; credits strained beyond the limit of safety; a growth of the desire for big profits at the expense of conservative business methods.

3.—DULL BUSINESS.—The cause of this has been so fully considered in the course of this treatise that it seems only necessary to say: If it is not due to the absence of any one of the known essentials to prosperity, enumerated in Chapter 7, it is due to Impair Savings.

* * * * * * * *

The conditions set forth under Point 1 are conducive not only to a healthy state of business, but they also favor stability. Those set forth under Point 2 tend toward extremes—too much business at one time, too little at another.

At "normal" times business ought to be of the character stated under Point 1; but we generally find much of a co-admixture of the conditions embraced in Points

2 and 3— on the one hand there is more or less of Impair Savings, as evidenced by the fact that the demand constantly falls short of the supply; on the other, we find a gradual but steady inflation going on, as evidenced by the constant swelling of the volume of circulating money, and much more so of bank money.[5] The latter especially has, in the last decade, expanded to an extent which seems to bring us near the limit. It has stimulated business while it went on; but in future we may have to do without this unhealthy stimulant, and if so, we may not again experience such a period of excessive boom as we did of late.

Let it be well understood, the phenomenal business activity witnessed in the United States, between 1897 and 1907, was largely caused by the phenomenal inflation of the bank money. While all economists admit the stimulating effect of an inflation of the currency, and while but few of them will attribute a similar (though weaker) influence to the inflation of bank money, such influence certainly existed, as explained on page 161. Also in Germany has the inflation of the bank money played its part towards creating the unusual business activity witnessed there in recent years and the aftermath will be severe, considering that the country has not (like the United States) many opportunities left for the profitable investment of savings[1] and that the latter, therefore, will largely assume the character of Impair Savings; far more so than with us. In either case the position as to foreign trade and as to the "balance of payments" has become rather weak, America exporting gold, and Germany struggling to retain her gold supply by means of a high bank rate. If the inflation-stimulant should spread to other countries, already weak in foreign trade, like Russia or Austria, it probably will not develop very much before the growing "balance of payments" inaugurates a drain on the gold supply, therewith deranging the country's financial condition and making an end to the inflation business.

ECONOMIC FALLACIES.

There is no science which contains so many contradictions and conflicting views as may be found in economics. Hardly two experts will everywhere agree on fundamental points and on their bearing. To a large extent this dissension of views is due to the fact that the origin of one of the most important phenomena, namely, depression and slack business, has so far remained unknown—in consequence of which every economist, who did his own thinking, formulated a theory of his own to account for those phenomena, and in doing so had to resort to more or less "adjustment" in order to make the facts agree with his theory. The true cause of depression known, we will have a guide for testing many of the conflicting opinions as to their correctness, and a number of views now current will have to be abandoned or modified. In the following I enumerate some of these:

1.—"*Extravagance is one of the chief causes of our present depression and of depressions in general.*—Had we had less extravagance, or, what comes to the same thing, more saving, at the time of the boom, less of the people's income would have been spent for commodities, and more of it for new constructions. Then the proportion between "Constructive" and "Commodity" Working Forces[7], instead of being as 15 to 85, might have been as 20 to 80. In consequence, new constructions would have proceeded at a still faster rate, and we would have arrived all the sooner at a superfluity of these, i. e., at a superfluity of productive capital. Then new constructions would come to a halt, the boom would cease, and depression would set in. The depression would not only set in so much the sooner, but would be more severe, with consumption restricted (as premised) and the number of unemployed Constructive Forces much larger than at present.

In a healthy development an increase of consumption should go hand in hand with the increase of productive capital. To restrict the former would mean a restriction of the demand. The lack of demand, however, is just what causes the depression.

2.—*Excessive extravagance during the boom was evidenced by the excessive demand for consumptibles, which was almost greater than the productive power of the country. Therefore that scarcity of labor. Without this excessive demand, that mad rush for extending the productive capital in order to meet the great demand would not have developed.* — No doubt the scarcity of labor indicated an unusual demand for the products of labor, i. e., for consumptibles. But I have shown, on page 161, that this great demand for labor was principally caused by the inflation of bank money.[5] A billion of additional bank money means a billion of additional demand for working forces. If the country's working forces represent a productive power of 20 billions per annum, and by means of inflation the demand is increased to 21 billions —not only the demand, but also the income and the buying power— then, indeed, the demand must seem unduly large when compared with the productive power. That excessive demand, however, as well as the seeming extravagance deduced therefrom, must disappear as soon as the inflation comes to a halt. The panic, therefore, was not caused by extravagance, but by the inflation of the bank money.

3.—*As we did not economize sufficiently during the boom, we must do so now; the greater the economy, the sooner shall we have the funds necessary for another era of new constructions.*—Do we really need more of new constructions at present and more economy to obtain the funds for erecting them, or do we need the reverse—less economy and more buying of consumptibles, so as to provide employment for the productive capital already existing? I believe we need the latter.

Though we often hear the assertion that we did not save enough and did not economize sufficiently during the boom, the fact remains that, despite the seeming extravagance, the country's aggregate savings were enormous—otherwise we would not have had the funds wherewith to create all those new constructions which sprung up at that time.

4.—*The panic was due to over-production.*—Previous to the panic the question was quite often raised as to whether over-production was really going on, and the question has as often been denied by all unbiased observers. Production did not run ahead of the demand but merely followed it. For the cause of the great demand I refer to Point 2.

5.—*Panics are due to a lack of equilibrium in production.*—This easy to say, but hard to prove. I have discussed this topic on page 70. As a rule, production will follow the demand, and if so, how can there be a lack of equilibrium in production?

6.—*Panics are caused by too rapidly "discounting" the future through placing of capital (cash capital) in fixed investments.*—So long as the funds used for fixed investments, i. e., for new constructions, like railroads, factories, etc., come from the saving process, there is no harm. And no harm if the funds are borrowed, provided the lender derives them, directly or indirectly, from the saving process. But the danger commences (even for solid undertakings) if the funds are derived from the inflation process—say, by extending the issue of bank money.[5] Inflation has that peculiar quality of being self-sustaining; the more there is of it, the more is needed (see page 163). And as inflation cannot be carried on indefinitely, a collapse is bound to ensue.

7.—*The panic was due, in part at least, to the inelasticity of our currency volume, which fails to respond to the varying demands of business. To remedy this, bank notes should be freely issued or retired according to the requirements of the money market.*—If, before the panic, our currency had been given the right kind of elasticity, the panic would most likely have been prevented—say, by allowing the issue of an emergency currency, subject to a high tax. But suppose that the tax had been low, and the notes issuable ad libitum, even at the time of the boom, what would have been the consequence? In face of the insatiable demand for cash funds which ruled in 1906 and 1907, we would have had an inflation of the currency (see page 169), on top of the inflation of the bank money. Then the collapse inevitably following excessive inflation might have led to a similar distrust of bank notes as did attach to the bank money, thus multiplying disaster.

Inflation for the sake of temporary needs, say, for moving the crops, does no harm, if followed by a corresponding contraction. Inflation, however, if resorted to in order to provide the funds for permanent investment, is objectionable. It over-stimulates the general demand while going on, but creates a shortage of demand when coming to a halt. (See Point 2.)

8.—*While at a time of great prosperity savings funds are absorbed almost exclusively in new constructions, an occasional setback be-*

comes necessary to provide for the money markets "other requirements."—These "other requirements" are a myth. In Chapter 2 I have discussed all imaginable possibilities as to what they might consist of, and have shown that none of them really absorb the country's savings funds.

9.—*No harm can attach to the saving process so long as the savings funds find ready employment. Even at times of depression they accumulate in the money market to a limited extent only, showing that they are absorbed. And as business men when absorbing them will apply them to some useful purpose, the saving process must always lead to a useful end.*—No argument has occasioned greater confusion in the economic world than this one, highly plausible as it appears. As a matter of fact the seemingly "useful end" often consists of nothing but Impair Investments[8]—a form of investment which so far has remained unknown to our economists. Once it is known, Argument 9 becomes untenable.

10.—*Savings funds, if failing to find useful employment at home, would simply go abroad.*—Except to a very limited extent investments abroad can not be effected unless the state of the country's foreign trade allows of it, the foreign investments being circumscribed by the extent to which the trade balance (see page 135) may be favorable—a subject fully elaborated on page 134.

11.—*Though the saving process may cause a shortage of demand at one time, say, during a depression, the shortage will be compensated for when the savings funds subsequently come to be invested.*—This view, though running counter to the one discussed under Point 9, is often heard. Both views are wrong. If working forces[6] are thrown out of employment, owing to lack of demand caused by the saving process, and are kept idle for any length of time, the productive power thus annihilated is lost forever, and is not compensated for by the fact that those working forces may find employment again later on.

12.—*Trade reactions are necessary evils, bound to recur in rotation.*—If we should ever be able to guard against Impair Savings, we would have the means of doing away with those extended periods of depression, and the belief in the inherent necessity of their recurrence would prove fallacious.

* * * * * * * *

In the foregoing I have discussed some of the views now current on extravagance, economy, saving and some other factors in connection with their bearing on our economic status. Most of our economists believe that the more we save (without hoarding) the better we are protected against depressions and disturbances. In contrast with this belief I maintain that if at times of depression or of slackening business we could check the saving process, and could enforce more buying and less accumulation on the part of the wealthy, we therewith could check the depression. On the whole our saving power is too large. In busy seasons too much is accumulated and invested in new constructions, the latter fact again increasing the business activity. If at such times we had more consumption and less saving, and consequently less of new constructions, the cycle of prosperity would last longer. We would not so quickly arrive at a period of superfluity of productive capital, with a consequent lull in new constructions and a change of the saving process from the Capitalistic to the Impairing Form.

If we could find a practicable method for controlling and eventually limiting the saving activity, things would soon shape themselves so as to conform to that healthy state of business described on page 180. The demand for working forces will then be as large as the supply; there will be employment for practically all of them; the feverish activity during a boom and the subsequent period of stagnation will be supplanted by a uniformly brisk state of business; the shifting and changing about of working forces[6] will give way to a greater stability of employment; of the working forces, fewer would be engaged in new constructions and more in the production of commodities, which would mean a larger allotment of the fruits of labor to each individual, i. e., a higher degree of prosperity.

Temporary economic disturbances may not be entirely eliminated, but protracted periods of depression would become impossible.

* * * * * * * *

ONCE MORE, THE "NEGLECTED POINT."

It was not my intention when writing this book to present a complete treatise on panics and depressions, following up their origin, development and gradual abatement. All that I have aimed at has been to bring out the "Neglected Point," and I have branched out on other subjects (for instance, the various depression theories) no further than necessary to elucidate my own views and defend my position. The object of this book is to reveal the dual nature of the saving process, its beneficent as well as its impairing form, and to bring out the main features of the latter—notably that strange duplex action which, on the one hand, places investment-seeking cash funds in the possession of the savers, while on the other it creates market conditions which open up opportunities for the investment of those funds—this at a time when the legitimate field of investment (new constructions, etc.) narrows down.

My investigations do not verify the universal belief that in the end the saving activity will always benefit the commonwealth as well as the individual saver. I have shown that it is far from being an unmixed blessing. It may harm as well as benefit the community. It will either stimulate business activity or depress it; either enliven the demand, or diminish it. If it ceases to be useful it at once becomes harmful. In its effects it is either constructive or destructive, never neutral.

* * * * * * * *

Before we can find the proper remedy for depressions, we must know their cause. I have stated, in this book, what I believe to be their true cause.

As a rule, the reader will not consider a depression theory complete unless it gives suggestions as to the remedy; such, however, I am not prepared to offer. But I dare say, if my depression theory should be accepted as the correct one, a remedy will be discovered. And even if a sweeping remedy for Impair Savings could not be found, the knowledge of their existence and of the harm they entail upon us, would go far in guiding us to shape our economic policy, wherever legislative measures have to be taken that bear upon the subject.

EXPLANATORY NOTES.

1st.—In this treatise the term "savings" is meant to cover all surplus earnings: those of the millionaire as well as those of the working man.

2nd.—The term "capital" should always be understood in the economic sense, meaning productive capital, or capital goods, like factories, houses, railroads, ships, etc. In common usage the term is often applied to cash funds, such as are loanable or available for investment. Wherever the latter kind of capital is referred to in this book, it will be called "cash capital."

3rd.—The terms "new constructions," "new wealth," or "additional wealth," are largely identical with "new productive capital," but they also include new acquisitions of what may be termed "unproductive capital," such as houses occupied by the owners, hospitals, schools, bridges, streets, pleasure boats and vehicles, and many kinds of constructions not intended for business purposes, in fact, all property left in the possession of the community at the end of the year *in addition* to what it possessed at the beginning of the year.

4th.—The term "money market" should be understood to include not only loanable funds, but all funds available for investment in new enterprises. It does not include, however, the liquid capital employed by business men in carrying on their regular business; such funds are not available for new enterprises, nor for loaning purposes.

5th.—By "Bank Money" is meant the deposits of business men and others in commercial banks, subject to check; their "money in bank." It does not include deposits in savings banks. In the United States it would include deposits in National banks, State banks, and most of those held by Trust banks.

6th.—The term "working forces" should be understood to mean only *individuals*, such as are engaged, directly or indirectly, in the production and distribution of commodities or in the creation of any kind of wealth; workingmen as well as men of other vocations—manufacturers, farmers, merchants, transporters, capitalists, etc. In fact, all men who derive an income from their being connected with a particular trade should be considered as constituting the working forces engaged in such trade to the extent of that income; even the capitalist who merely draws interest on the funds which he advances to participants in that trade.

7th.—The term "Constructive Working Forces" refers to such individuals as are engaged, directly or indirectly, in new constructions or in the creation of additional wealth;[3] whereas those who are engaged in the production of commodities intended for consumption are referred to as "Commodity Working Forces." This distinction does not exclude the possibility that one and the same man, for instance a dealer, may partly belong in the one class and partly in the other.

8th.—The term "Impairing Form of Investment" has been chosen to indicate that an impairment of the community's welfare is intimately connected with that form of investment. But it should be understood that the *act of investing*, as such, is not the cause of the impairment; on the contrary, the act of investing is always beneficial to the welfare of the community. The impairment comes from some other cause, as explained in Chapter 5, not from the investment.

9th.—The term ' impoverishment" should not be understood to mean reduction to poverty, but merely "becoming poorer." A man may become impoverished by $1000 and still be a rich man.

10th.—The term "alienation of property" should be understood in a broad sense and to include not only the selling of property in cases of urgent need, but also the borrowing on it, say, in the shape of a mortgage or other pledge; and the term "borrowing" ("borrower") should also be understood to cover both, borrowing as well as selling. A very familiar instance where a man borrows on his property, or even on mere credit, is furnished by the "running behind" of a business man who does not earn his expenses in times of depression and whose balance-sheet at the end of the year shows a loss where it used to show a surplus. Such loss reduces his wealth; and unless he allows his plant or his stock to run down, others will gain what he loses. If at the end of the year he has less money on hand, others have so much more; if his outstanding accounts have become smaller, the community owes him so much less and has become relatively richer; if he has more notes outstanding, those who hold the notes have acquired a kind of lien on his property (which amounts to an alienation on his part) and at the same time have found investment for their funds when buying those notes. Just so if the State's income runs behind in years of general depression, and if bonds are issued to make up for the deficit; this gives the savers an opportunity for investing their surplus earnings; but to the same extent the community becomes indebted; i. e., poorer.